Science Fiction, Science Fact!
Ages 8–12

Science Fiction, Science Fact! Ages 8–12 is a book for story-loving primary teachers who want to find a creative way to teach science. Contextualising science in a story that pupils know and love, the book contains a wide range of activities and investigations to help Key Stage 2 pupils engage in science learning, while also extending aspects of the English national curriculum.

The book offers valuable support to busy teachers and, by ensuring science lessons are enjoyable and accessible for pupils, helps children get involved in investigations in a way that is memorable for them. Using coloured illustrations and diagrams throughout, the book contains:

- the relevant scientific context alongside a link to one of six exciting children's stories;
- clever and unique suggestions to 'storify the science';
- instructions for teachers to give to their pupils;
- tips on how to deliver the lesson in an immersive way;
- guidance on assessing pupils' level of understanding.

Science Fiction, Science Fact! Ages 8–12 is packed full of ideas for weaving science into cross-curricular lessons, and is an invigorating and essential resource for Key Stage 2 teachers and science co-ordinators seeking to inject some creativity into their science lessons.

Jules Pottle is a primary science specialist teacher with experience teaching in primary schools for over twenty years, and a trainer for Storytelling Schools, UK. She won the Primary Science Teaching Trust's Primary Science Teacher of the Year in 2015.

Science Fiction, Science Fact! Ages 8–12

Learning Science through Well-Loved Stories

Jules Pottle

Routledge
Taylor & Francis Group

LONDON AND NEW YORK

First published 2018
by Routledge
2 Park Square, Milton Park, Abingdon, Oxon OX14 4RN

and by Routledge
711 Third Avenue, New York, NY 10017

Routledge is an imprint of the Taylor & Francis Group, an informa business

© 2018 Jules Pottle

The right of Jules Pottle to be identified as author of this work
has been asserted by her in accordance with sections 77 and
78 of the Copyright, Designs and Patents Act 1988.

All rights reserved. No part of this book may be reprinted
or reproduced or utilised in any form or by any electronic,
mechanical, or other means, now known or hereafter
invented, including photocopying and recording, or in any
information storage or retrieval system, without permission in
writing from the publishers.

Trademark notice: Product or corporate names may be
trademarks or registered trademarks, and are used only for
identification and explanation without intent to infringe.

British Library Cataloguing-in-Publication Data
A catalogue record for this book is available from the British Library

Library of Congress Cataloging-in-Publication Data
A catalog record has been requested for this book

ISBN: 978-1-138-29093-8 (hbk)
ISBN: 978-1-138-29094-5 (pbk)
ISBN: 978-1-315-26581-0 (ebk)

Typeset in Helvetica
by Florence Production Limited, Stoodleigh, Devon, UK

For my lovely mum who was always on the sidelines, cheering. And my dad, whose enthusiasm for science built the foundations of this book.

Contents

Acknowledgements

With love and gratitude to my wonderful and very patient family who supported me while I was writing.

Thanks to Alex Sinclair for his hours of editing and excellent advice on all things scientific.

Thanks to Sarah Bearchell (*Sarah's Adventure in Science*) for her ideas and enthusiasm.

Thanks also to Dona Foster and the Modernising Medical Microbiology research group at Nuffield Department of Clinical Medicine, University of Oxford, who gave me practical advice on microbes.

And finally, thanks to Rufus Cooper for his amazing illustrations, which have brought this book to life.

My thanks are also due to the following publishers and authors for permission to include materials in the text:

Random House Children's Books for excerpt from *The Golden Compass: His Dark Materials* by Philip Pullman, copyright © 1995 by Philip Pullman. Used by permission of Alfred A. Knopf, an imprint of Random House Children's Books, a division of Penguin Random House LLC. All rights reserved.

Scholastic Ltd for excerpt from *Northern Lights*, text copyright © Philip Pullman, 1998, reproduced by permission of Scholastic Ltd. All rights reserved.

David Higham Associates Limited and Penguin Books Ltd for extract from *Charlie and the Chocolate Factory* by Road Dahl. Text copyright © 1964 Roald Dahl. Published by Penguin Books Ltd and used with permission.

Thanks also to the following groups who have given me permission to use ideas from their websites:

Royal Society of Chemistry (n.d.). *Mission: Starlight – A global experiment on UV protection*. From The Royal Society of Chemistry: www.rsc.org

The Science Museum. (n.d.). *Rocket Mice*. From Science Museum: www.sciencemuseum.org.uk

Introduction

Why do you need this book?

Science is a crucial part of every child's education.

It engages children in thinking about how things work, it encourages them to be observant and notice patterns, it teaches them to be curious and prompts them to ask pertinent questions that can be tested. We need these skills to be creative, to visualise and, ultimately, to persevere in problem solving.

And yet, primary science is often a second class citizen. It rarely takes centre stage in the primary classroom as the 'real business of the day'. English and maths dominate the timetable. For many primary teachers, for many reasons, science is a hard subject to tackle.

But everybody loves a good story.

What if you could put a story at the centre of your teaching and have the science and the English tumble out of it?

This book is written for story lovers and for those who find science a little bewildering or dry. It takes the wonder of a good story and helps you to use that story world as a context for science teaching.

I have tried to provide everything you'll need to know about the science as well as the practicalities of setting up the lesson, linking it to the book. There are also ways to record the learning so that you can pick up the book, grab the equipment and run with it!

Why use stories?

Stories create a context for the science. We use science all the time in the real world. To drive a car we need sufficient friction in the tread in our tyres and sufficient thrust from the engine. When you teach science in context, it makes more sense. It stops being an abstract concept (of friction or thrust) and becomes something the children can visualise (the grip on the road or the acceleration of the car).

It helps to put the science into the context of a real world but it could also be a fictional world. What is important is that the world is clear in the mind of the child. In a story, there are also characters with problems to solve. The science is important to the characters so, if we are engaged with the emotions of the characters, then the science becomes important to us.

There are lots of benefits to using stories in education and many studies show that context-based science teaching can be very successful. My experience has shown that it engages children who love science anyway (the non-fiction readers and the factual answer seekers) and it engages the story lovers (the huge novel readers who can suspend reality and live in an entirely fictional world). It seems to cover all the bases.

I once had a child in my class who loved science but wasn't keen on English. During creative writing sessions, his head would be on the desk and the paper would be blank. But during science lessons he was wide awake and thinking, joining in discussions and asking interesting questions. He would only write two lines of story in his English book but he'd write two pages of witty and entertaining story in his science book. Using stories can hook the story lovers into science but it also hooks the science lovers into stories.

How do we use the book?

First, I suggest you read the next chapter, as it will help you set out a lesson that is playful and engaging. There are tips in that chapter that will help you in all your science teaching.

The next six chapters cover six stories. Each story is used to teach one science topic. The level of science has been matched to the difficulty of the text so that easier texts cover easier science concepts. I have also included one picture book for the younger end of this age range and one topic that is skills based rather than content driven (*Alice's Adventures in Wonderland*).

I have ordered the science so that the things you teach at the start of the topic are taught through the first chapters of the book so that you can start reading the book to your class at the start of the term and move forwards through the story as you move forwards through the science topic.

The books and topics included in this book are as shown on the facing page.

Of course, there are lots of books that lend themselves to the teaching of science. I hope you will go out and find more. I chose these ones as they offered links to complete topics rather than bits and pieces from all over the curriculum and because I love these stories.

So, choose a book or choose the science topic and turn to the relevant chapter. I suggest you read the whole chapter before you start teaching and check that you have the equipment you need. You may want to use all the lessons or you may want to dip into them. Use the book as you see fit.

You may want to teach extra lessons alongside the ones in this book, to supplement the children's learning. You may want to explain everything in the science sections to them or just give them what they are ready to digest and understand. You know your class. You'll know when they've understood the science.

You may be working from a different curriculum and only some of the lessons fit your needs. Take the ones that work and invent your own to fit the rest.

I hope it inspires you to get the next generation excited about science.

Novel	Storyline	Science concepts
The Black Rabbit By Philippa Leathers (a picture book)	A rabbit is being followed by a big black rabbit who seems rather threatening. But it is the big black rabbit who comes to the rescue in the end.	Light including: • We need light in order to see • Light sources and reflective surfaces • Transparent and opaque materials • Changing shadows
The Last Wild by Piers Torday	Almost all the animals in the world (except the pests) have been wiped out by a disease. One boy must find a way to save the last few left – the last wild.	Living things including humans: • Grouping animals • Biological keys • Food chains • Interdependence • Digestion • Teeth • Vaccinations
Charlie and the Chocolate Factory by Roald Dahl	Charlie's family are close to starving when he wins a trip inside the famous chocolate factory and discovers all the wonders inside.	Changing materials: • Melting • (Thermal insulation) • Reversible and irreversible changes • Chemical changes • Burning • Dissolving • Factors that affect the speed of dissolving
Kensuke's Kingdom by Michael Morpurgo	A young boy and his dog are washed up on the shores of a desert island. He has to learn to survive with the help of Kensuke, a Japanese soldier, shipwrecked years before and now living among and protecting the animals on the island.	Changes in state and the water cycle: • Solids liquids and gases • Changes in state • Capillary action • Evaporation and condensation • The water cycle • Burning
The Northern Lights by Philip Pullman	When the mysterious Gobblers kidnap her friend Roger, Lyra embarks on a journey to the frozen North to save him.	Forces: • Gravity • Balanced and unbalanced forces • Friction • Air resistance • Upthrust in the air
Alice's Adventures in Wonderland by Lewis Carroll	Alice falls down the rabbit hole and into Wonderland. She wants to follow the white rabbit into the beautiful garden beyond the door but a series of events and bizarre characters distract her.	Science skills: • Testing against a control • Estimating and predicting • Changing one variable at a time • Setting up comparative investigations • Finding all the possible solutions • Planning an investigation and controlling variables

1 How to teach a great science lesson

Science lessons should be a real highlight in your week: a chance to be playful and have some fun, a chance to let the children lead their own learning and an opportunity to inject a little awe and wonder. This book gives you all the knowhow you'll need to plan a really exciting lesson, set in the context of a story.

In this chapter, I will share with you some of the tricks of the trade that I have learned through 20-odd years of teaching primary science. They can be summarised as:

- You don't have to know everything
- Be playful
- Talk about it so you can think about it
- Write about it in a focussed and creative way
- Let the children discover it for themselves
- Feel the science
- A little suspense is very engaging
- Put the science in context.

You may find it useful to read this chapter first.

You don't have to know everything

Most primary school teachers have a degree in humanities or arts. Very few have a science degree or even science A levels so it is very common for primary teachers to feel daunted by the thought of teaching science. You are not alone! We have all experienced the hand going up and the question that we just can't answer. I have two stock replies in those circumstances:

- Great question! I have no idea – I'll find out.
- I think this is what happens but I'll check and get back to you.

They both involve a quick conversation with 'Professor Google' (who knows pretty much everything) after the lesson and then a quick return to the question at the start of the next lesson. Remember that your job is to encourage the children to be curious so embrace their questions and be content to discover the answers together. Even great scientists would be keen to tell us that they don't know all the answers!

The point of a primary science lesson is to promote scientific thinking. Very few children will remember every fact that they learned in primary science lessons but they will remember the lesson where they made pop rockets and worked out how to make them go really high. They will remember being allowed to plant their bean seeds in purple paint just to see whether they grew purple plants. Hopefully, they will leave primary school thinking science is fun and knowing how to set up an experiment to test out a question to satisfy their own curiosity. So, you don't need to be the person who knows everything. You just need to be the person who is willing to help the children find their own answers.

Be playful

Being playful in science lessons is crucial. It is what engages the children. If you give off an air of wonder and excitement about finding out what happens, you'll find it's contagious.

The best lessons are the ones where the children are excited about the science. Yes, they'll get overexcited sometimes and yes, it might be both messy and noisy. But a lesson where all the children are making a mess and making a noise, while completely engaged in the task, and being delighted by their own results, is the epitome of good science teaching.

Be prepared to try out their ideas – they'll love you for it. I once set the children a problem as part of a 'separating materials topic'. I mixed rice, steel paper clips and marbles into a tub of water and challenged them to separate out all the elements. I was expecting them to suggest sieves or magnets as a method of separating the items but children are full of surprises. One child suggested that if you launched the tub upwards a few feet, the items would leap upwards out of the water and the water would remain in the tub. I could see this wouldn't work. The other children in the class could see this wouldn't work! But the child who suggested it clearly had a misconception that he needed to test out. So, I let him. We took the tub outside and had a go. It was a fairly controlled launch but it was still a pretty wet experience and the items all stayed mixed in the water! But it was safe, the children remembered it, the misconception was dealt with . . . and we all had fun. I could have simply told him that it wouldn't work but he wouldn't have believed it, without testing it. This is why it is important to have a playful attitude as the teacher.

Sometimes, being playful means being prepared to put on a bit of a show for the children: making the rocket go really high (without showing them how you did it) or pretending you're surprised when your specially weighted cake-tin rolls uphill instead of down.

Play can also be the process of fiddling about with something to see what happens or to see how it works or to make it work better. Great scientists, such as Watson and Crick, who discovered the double helix shape of the molecule DNA (and thus revealed the process by which DNA is replicated) refer to the process they used as 'play': Watson wrote 'All we had to do was to construct a set of molecular models and begin to play' (Watson, 1968, pp. 50–1). Some people refer to this process as tinkering. Whatever you call it, we need more of it in the primary classroom.

So, encourage playfulness in your classroom and watch the curiosity, creativity and engagement grow.

Talk about it so you can think about it

Science talk is really important. If you give the children time to express their thoughts about what is happening (or what might happen) then you give them time to frame their ideas in their own minds. Talking to another child can also help raise differences in their understanding, which can then be debated and misconceptions can be tackled.

In this book, I give you ways to lead the children to their own answers through discussion. Try not to give them the answer at the start. If you tell them the science, they hear it but they may not process it. In my experience, as it is not their own discovery, they are less likely to engage with it. If you ask them to explain their own idea and they find out they were right – then they have a sense of achievement and delight in the science. In the same way, if they voice a misconception and then find out that the science works in a way they hadn't anticipated, then they are more likely to relearn the science without the misconception. Talking about what might happen helps them to engage with the science so learning can take place.

Science talk needs to leave room for lots of ideas, even if the ideas are not correct. It is all too easy to close down a discussion with the right answer and end the discussion. This stops learning in its tracks. Imagine this situation: a teacher hears a child ask an interesting question – 'Will that puddle freeze if I put an ice cube into it?'

The teacher knows the answer. By answering 'No'. she ends the discussion and the child won't have a chance to explore his idea so she chooses to say something else – 'Shall we try it and find out?' Now, there is some engagement with the science. Ice cubes are gathered and the child can put one in the puddle. He discovers that the puddle doesn't freeze. The teacher could leave it there. But if she acts a little surprised and seems curious then she could show the child how to ask further questions such as 'Do we need more ice?' or 'What happens to the ice when you put it in the puddle?' and thus the engagement with the science can be prolonged and developed until the child is able to have some first-hand experience and is able to answer his own question for himself.

Scientific thinking can be shut down in a classroom where the teacher asks the children what they think is happening and stops asking for responses at the first right answer. Once the right answer is confirmed as the right answer, the thinking stops.

So, wherever you are able, keep the talk going, maintain that debate and let the children vocalise their ideas whether they be right or wrong. Then, let them experience the science and discuss it again. And only when all the children have engaged with the discussion lead them through the correct scientific explanation – using the words of the children and the correct scientific vocabulary, side by side.

If you need to get more out of the children without giving away what is right or wrong, you can always say 'Tell me more'.

I was recently involved in a really interesting piece of research that has resulted in some excellent teacher training. Helen Wilson of Oxford Brookes University and Bridget Holligan of Science Oxford decided to test out the idea that stretching the children's minds in science lessons with 'Big Questions' and discussion could have a positive impact on their ability to problem solve in other subjects. They set up the Thinking, Doing, Talking Science Project based on the following idea:

> Professor Philip Adey has made the important point that 'What the research shows consistently is that if you face children with intellectual challenges and then help them talk through the problems towards a solution, then you almost literally stretch their minds. They become cleverer, not only in the particular topic, but across the curriculum.' It can therefore be argued that teachers cannot afford to allow their pupils to miss out on the opportunities for deep thinking.

One method of ensuring this is to incorporate a 'Bright Ideas' slot into lessons and this need not take more than ten minutes per session. Science is surely all about thinking and the enjoyment of thinking deeply. Discussing big ideas is more important than finding the right answer and it will obviously be important to establish a classroom atmosphere in which all ideas and responses will be valued.

(Coates and Wilson, 2003)

So, I would encourage you to include games that encourage talk into your science lessons. They will show you what the children already know, highlight misconceptions and provide a safe platform for them to practise making suggestions, thinking out loud, debating or putting forward ideas, in front of their peers.

Write about it in a focussed and creative way

Every school has their own policy on what should be recorded in a science lesson. Some require all science to be recorded in a full write-up after every session. That might include:

- *Question*: Which ice lolly lasts the longest in the hot sun?
- *Equipment*: Draw the equipment you used and label it.
- *Method*: Explain how you set up the equipment and how you took the measurements.
- *Prediction*: Which ice lolly you think will melt first and why?
- *Results*: Table of results (time and length) and line graph with 3 lines – one for each lolly (time and length).
- *Conclusion*: Name the lolly that lasts the longest and explain why.
- *Evaluation*: How could I improve upon my test design?

This is a long laborious process and is likely to take longer than the practical work.

While I agree that children need to know **how to write** each section of a full science report, I don't think they need to write **every part**, every week.

Consider the amount of time that you are allotted to teach science every week. At least half of it should be practical work. Some of it will be needed for settling the children, introducing the topic and engaging the children in the science they are about to do. So, that doesn't leave hours at the end of the lesson for writing about it. So, what do we do?

- Use maths lessons
- Use English lessons
- And use the science lessons!

First, if you plan well in advance, you can use maths lessons to record the data and convert measurements from one unit to another etc. Embed your maths lesson within the science lesson and use the science data to teach the maths.

Likewise, you can use English lessons to write about what you have learned and I give lots of examples about how to do that in this book. After each lesson described, you'll find suggestions on how to record the children's learning in English lessons where you may be studying a particular form of writing such as play-scripts or explanations. If you are using the story as the centre of your cross-curricular planning then why not make your recording of the science cross-curricular too?

But what should we record in the science lessons themselves? Always write about what you found out (an explanation of what happened with reference to the science) but it need only be a sentence long. In addition, you could choose one of the parts of a full write-up to do after each lesson (e.g. a prediction). Make sure you choose each one at least once per topic and aim to let the children do this unaided on a regular basis, so you can assess what they are able to do.

If you want to record your findings in a creative way then you could:

- focus on predictions (write them before you start the practical work) and, at the end, say whether you were correct;
- focus on writing instructions and write a clear method with diagrams of the equipment;
- focus on collecting data – draw up your own table and graph the data;
- focus on conclusions and write a detailed, scientific explanation of what happened, including diagrams;
- focus on the design of your experiment. Draw the equipment you used and annotate it. At the end of the session, evaluate the design of your experiment;
- write a full report, including all the elements.

Of course, you may need a quick drawing, a photo or a clear title on the page so the children remember what they have done in each lesson but writing a whole report every time turns the science lesson into an English lesson and valuable science learning time is lost.

Let the children discover it for themselves

If you present a child with some science in an authoritative 'this is how it works' voice, you are showing them **your** science. It is not **their** science. They may be interested or they may not be. However, if you let the children discover the science, then they own it. They own it in the same way that they own that den that they built at lunchtime!

So, when you start something new with the children, give them time to explore. Give them time to play. If you are investigating forces, spend half a lesson playing with cars and ramps. Then, when they have built speed bumps to slow the cars down and tried really steep slopes to make them go further, then, they'll have their own ideas about what question they would like to investigate in a fair test. They'll be investigating their own idea – they'll own it.

Likewise, if you give them the wires, the bulbs and the batteries and ask them to make the bulb light, without further instructions, then, they'll discover it for themselves. When the first children to get it to light, for a moment, they are the resident experts and they 'own the knowledge'. Then, as others work it out, they own it too. I live for that triumphant 'YES!' that you hear when the children get something to happen. You don't get that by showing them how to do it.

It might take a while but this time is not wasted. Many great scientists discovered a great many things that didn't work before they discovered the one that did!

So, make time for play in the primary classroom. Give the children time to handle equipment before they have to use it to collect data. Let them see what happens so that they can come up with their own ideas that they are motivated to test out. Let them discover science for themselves. Yes, this may take a little longer but, as Johnston (2004) explains in the following article, the time spent on letting children discover the science for themselves pays dividends in terms of engagement in the science.

> It seems that in busy primary classrooms the opportunities to observe and to develop observation skills can easily be overlooked, but finding time for children to observe phenomena and to follow their own interests will pay dividends in supporting quality outcomes in all areas of scientific enquiry and understandings. In a discovery approach, the outcomes will be greater in terms of all enquiry skills, as well as understandings and attitudes, where the children:
>
> * are central to the learning;
> * explore and discover things about the world around them that arise from their own initial curiosity and observations;
> * construct their own understandings through their observation and exploration;
> * are supported by teachers and peers through social interaction.
>
> (Johnston, 2004, p. 21)

Feel the science

Science lessons should be as practical as your space and equipment will allow.

Upthrust is the force that holds up a boat when it is floating. We can tell children it is there but it remains as an abstract idea until we can get them to feel it. If you ask a child to submerge a football in a large tank of water, they will be able to feel how hard it is to submerge the football and feel the upthrust pushing it back up. Now they can feel the upthrust it's is no longer just an arrow on your diagram on the board – it is real.

Children are much more likely to retain information if they have seen it happen or felt it with their own hands.

Misconceptions often happen because the children haven't experienced the science at first hand. Imagine giving a class some objects and asking them to test whether they will float or sink. A common misconception is that heavy things sink and light ones float. If you include some surprising objects in the selection you can get the children to test out their misconceptions and come to a better understanding. Surprising objects might be: pumice stone which floats (stones normally sink), different plastics (some float and some sink), aluminium block and aluminium take-away-container/drinks can (only the one with air inside will float). In an activity like this, you'll find the surprising items are the ones that get all the attention and generate a lot of talk.

Practical science lessons do require equipment and primary schools often work on a tight budget and don't have large sets of science equipment. But you can do a lot of science with household objects so you'll find you can do many of the experiments suggested in this book without specialist equipment.

With a rowdy class, prone to messing about with equipment, I have found the trick is to move fast. Stop the process when one or two groups have gathered some useable data. Give a few warnings before you stop so that everyone knows to speed up. But stop before there are children with time on their hands to think about ways to mess about with the equipment!

You can also have an extra extension task to hand to occupy the very speedy group – there's always one.

A little suspense can be very engaging

Suspense is the key to a good science demonstration. What do I mean by a demonstration? In this book, I refer to a range of different types of lesson structures – activities, investigations and demonstrations.

- **Activity** – the children do or make something in order to 'feel the science' for themselves. Nothing is measured and no data is collected.
- **Investigation** – the children carry out some kind of test, make measurements and data is collected.
- **Demonstration (demos)** – the teacher shows the children something to capture their interest and spark discussion. It might be very quick or form the basis of a whole lesson.

During a demo, the teacher is leading the session from the front. Some demos are very quick and for this reason you need to get the maximum amount of engagement before you start the demo and suspense can be a great tool to grab their attention. Let me put this in context with a lesson you may have done yourself.

When I teach my first lesson on air resistance, the first thing I do is stand on a chair, holding out two identical pieces of A4 paper above the floor, parallel to the floor as they would be on a desk. This gets their attention, as I don't usually stand on the chairs.

I ask them which piece of paper will hit the ground first. One or two children immediately join in the game, shouting out their predictions. Not all the children have engaged with the science yet so I continue. I ask them to tell their partner what they think, then make a decision and put up their hands. At random, I ask them for their prediction. I give no more credence to the children who insist they are the same than to the children who make outlandish claims such as the one on the left is thicker. I say things like 'Interesting, yes maybe!'

I could do this until I have asked the entire class. But that may go on too long and some may then lose interest.

Somewhere after children begin to engage and before I bore or frustrate them, there is a sweet spot – a point where the maximum engagement happens. Children are giving me ideas. Children are interacting with each other's ideas. They are all looking at me and talking about the paper. At this point, I start a countdown. And when I get to 3, 2, 1, I screw up one of the sheets of paper into a tight ball and, while they're all protesting, I drop them both.

They all cared that I changed the rules at the last minute. They were all engaged. And they all note which paper hit the ground first.

Had I just dropped them at the start, only the few who engaged at the start would be really watching, or caring, as only they had already thought about what might happen.

Building the suspense, builds engagement. Magicians and street artists are masters of this art. They spend five minutes building to a trick that takes a few seconds. But everyone is looking and everyone is engaged by the time the actually do the trick and they get a good response.

The same thing works in science lessons.

- Get their attention, ask them to talk to a partner, to discuss and to predict and thus engage with the science.
- Don't let on who is right and who is wrong.
- You can even act as if you are about to start and then deliberately make a mistake (e.g. drop one sheet of paper rather than both). Children love to see the teacher mess up. That gets their full attention.
- Then, when you know you've got them – show them the science!

Put the science into context

Children understand the science most clearly, when they can see the practical application of the science: floating and sinking is clearly understood when you start building rafts to get off the desert island. This is what has led me to the teaching of science through stories. Once the child has engaged with the characters in the story and lived alongside them as you read, they care far more about whether that raft will float and carry the character home. It is unlikely, in our everyday lives, that we will need to solve a life or death problem by building a raft, so building a raft for a character (who is real in the imagination) is the next best thing.

Providing a context in which the science is useful is a way to engage the children.

This context needs to be real in the mind of the child but it doesn't have to be true! It could be fictional. Of course, fantasy stories where magic changes the way that the fantasy world operates might be muddling if used in this context but there are many fictional stories based in our world with science that operates in the same way as in the real world. Alternatively, there are also fantasy elements that can be challenged and tested to see whether they could work in the real world such as working out whether gobstoppers really can be everlasting. So, with a little careful treatment, many stories can provide a context for science investigations and they work well together.

As Pie Corbett beautifully put it, 'Without science we are lost. Without story we are trapped alone in the darkness of ourselves. For too long, these companions have wandered on separate tracks' (Smith and Pottle, 2015, p. ix).

The rest of this book is dedicated to the nuts and bolts of bringing science alive to children by engaging them with science in the context of a fictional world.

———————————————

2 *The Black Rabbit*

Philippa Leathers (2013)
(A picture book)

TOPIC PLANNER

Story link	Science: Light	Activity	Page
Darkness	How we see Solving problems – (tinkering)	Making a dark box (activity)	10
Shining eyes	Reflecting light Reflective materials vs light sources Predicting and testing	Light source or reflective? Sorting materials using the light box (investigation)	15–16
Dark shadows	Shadows Testing and finding an answer to a question	What is the best material for a shadow puppet? (investigation) Make a shadow puppet (activity)	19–20
The enormous black rabbit	How the size of a shadow changes Measuring, recording and spotting patterns	How do you make an enormous shadow? (investigation)	24–5
Too bright?	Blocking harmful light Designing a fair test Testing and drawing a conclusion	Looking after our eyes (investigation)	28

DARKNESS

Story link

The woods are dark.

THE SCIENCE: How we see

In order to see something, light has to get right inside our eyes and land on the layer of sensitive cells at the back, called the retina. The retina senses the light and sends messages to the brain about the light. The brain makes sense of these messages by turning them into the image that we see. There must be a hole in the eye for the light to get in and indeed there is: the black dot in the centre of our eyes, the pupil, is in fact a hole. There is a layer of transparent tissue over the top, like a window.

If there is no light going into our eyes, there is no light to sense so we see nothing. It is dark.

In our world of electrical gadgets we are rarely in complete darkness. Our eyes are very good at adapting to low light so children often think that they will be able to see objects in the dark, particularly brightly coloured ones.

It is very difficult to achieve total darkness in school, within the school day, so the best way to experience this is by making a sealed box with a peephole so that the children can see that it is totally dark inside the box and nothing can be seen.

ACTIVITY: Making a dark box

You will need:

- shoe boxes (or other boxes that can be opened and closed easily) – one per pair of children
- black gaffer tape (adults only) or black electrical tape
- masking tape
- sellotape
- black paper
- scissors
- bradawl (adults only)
- plastic model of the eye (available from educational suppliers).

Storify the science

Read the entire story to the children, spending time looking at the pictures. Ask the children to tell you what happened in the story. Listen out for mention of the shadows. Tell the children that you are going to be studying light and dark over the next few sessions.

Turn to the page where the rabbit first goes into the forest and notices his shadow has gone. Turn back to the first page where the rabbit is in the bright sunshine and flick through the rest of the book. Compare the picture of the dark wood to the rest of the scenes. Ask the children what they notice about the colours in the pictures. Elicit that the forest looks mostly brown and black, while the other pictures are full of green and yellow and blue etc.

Ask the children to look around them in the classroom. Ask them how it would look at night. Listen out for children who tell you that the colours might look different. Ask how they know and discuss experiences of being in the dark.

Ask whether anyone has ever been in total darkness. Ask them what it was like and listen to descriptions. They may well tell you that they can see very little in the dark. Accept all responses at this point without giving a correct answer.

Ask them how we could make the classroom totally dark. Listen to all the suggestions and agree that it might be really tricky.

Show them a dark box that you have made. Ask a child to look into the hole and describe what they can see. If you have made it well, and the child has their eye pressed up to the hole, they should say 'nothing'!

 ## Set the challenge

Your challenge is to make a totally dark space.

You are going to make a dark box. But you must make it totally dark when it is closed. We'll be using it to put things inside so it must have a lid or a flap so it can open and close.

When you make your dark box think about:

- how to seal up any cracks;
- how to open and close the box;
- how to make the box seal well (you may have to hold the lid or flap shut);
- where to put the peep hole.

Keep looking into your box to see whether you have made it totally dark.

Now gather some objects that might be in the forest: a stick, a blade of grass, a stone, a leaf or some bark.

Think about what you might see if you put them into the dark box.

Open your box and place these items inside. You could even glue them to the inside edges of the box, opposite the peephole. Close your box and look into it. What can you see?

Now open the lid/flap and look through the peep-hole. What can you see now?

Teacher's top tips

The object of this activity is to experience complete darkness. Without this experience, many children will hang onto the misconception that you can still see something in complete darkness.

One of the key skills here will be problem solving so try not to give them too many instructions. Just let them solve the problem of making the box dark, in their own way.

Let them try using clear sellotape, or masking tape so that they can see that the light must be completely blocked out. It doesn't matter how messy the boxes look, as long as the inside is totally dark. They may want to colour the inside black – again, let them.

Leave your dark box available for the children to look at while they are making theirs. They'll learn a lot by working out how you solved the problems they are facing.

They will need to cut a peephole. I suggest that you use a bradawl to poke a small hole in their box – let the children decide where the hole should be. Then show them how to carefully increase the size of the hole by pushing a pencil into the hole, then a larger barrelled object such as a paintbrush, until you have a hole about 1 cm across.

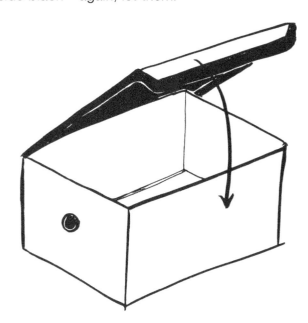

To seal the openings, cut a piece of black felt and stick it to the underside of the flap, hanging well over the edges. It will seal up the crack when the flap is closed.

What results should I expect?

The children make a dark box that doesn't let in any chinks of light. When an object is placed inside and the box closed, the object is not visible through the peep-hole as there is no light.

 ## Finale

Discuss with the children what they could see inside their dark box and any issues they had making it totally dark.

Discuss what the difference was with the box open. Elicit that when there is light, we can see. Without any light, we can see nothing. So light is very important in the process of seeing.

Ask the children to shut their eyes. Ask them why they can't see anything. Discuss how we need light and we need our eyes to be able to see. Explain that the light must go into our eyes through a tiny hole in order for us to see.

Ask the children to look at each other's eyes. Can they see a hole? Lead them to the idea that the pupil is a hole.

You could use a video or a model of an eye, at this point, to show them all the parts of the eye and how light reaches the retina.

Draw a diagram of a person looking at a lamp. Show the direction of the light as it travels INTO the eye. Children often draw this the wrong way around, with light travelling out of the person's eye. Draw the light ray with a ruler, emphasising that light travels in a straight line.

Keep your light boxes safe – you'll need them for the next activity.

 # What next?

If you want to record your findings in a creative way then you could:

- Write instructions for making a dark box.
- Role-play: being two rabbits. One explains to the other why it is dark in the forest.
- Write a letter to the rabbit, explaining why it is so dark in the forest.
- Draw a diagram of an eye, labelling the pupil and the retina. Show light rays going into the eye.
- Make a snakes and ladders style board game where you must creep from the start to the finish without being seen. Design it with dark squares showing somewhere to hide (such as a cave) and light squares where you'll be out in the open. Whenever you land on a square that is a bright place, such as an open meadow, you slide down a snake (because you can be seen there). Whenever you land on a dark place, such as a cave, you go up a ladder.

 # Assessing children's understanding

The following statement is an indicator of basic understanding:

- I can't see anything in the dark.

More advanced understanding:

- I can see because light goes into my eyes. If there is no light, I cannot see.
- Light rays go into my eyes through the pupil when I see something.

SHINING EYES

Story link

There are eyes in the forest.

THE SCIENCE: Reflecting light

Children often struggle to tell the difference between a light source that is giving out light, and something shiny, such as tinsel, that is merely reflecting the light.

Light sources give out light. In a dark room, we would see the light and any objects close enough to be lit up by the light. Light sources include the sun (our nearest star), other stars, electric lights, torches and flames.

If an object is not a light source, we can only see it because light reflects off that object. However, if the object has a smooth and shiny surface, light reflects off the surface in a very orderly way. This may make it sparkle. In fact, the light is so orderly in some reflections that we can actually see an image reflected, as in a mirror.

If you put a shiny glass bauble next to a fairy light, you can see the light reflecting from the shiny surface and the shiny surface appears to be giving out light like a light source. This is why children get confused as their experience tells them that some shiny things look as though they give out light.

There are other confusing materials such as glow in the dark stickers (which are actually a light source) and high visibility clothing (which is not a light source but is highly reflective).

If you put a bauble or a high visibility jacket in a dark box, you won't be able to see them as they are not giving out light. The best way to help children with these misconceptions is to give them first-hand experience of this.

The sun is a light source, as are the stars but the moon is not. The moon is made of rock and rock does not give out light. It merely reflects the bright light of the sun.

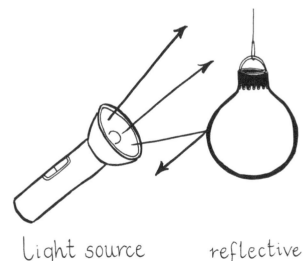

Light source   reflective

INVESTIGATION: Light source or reflective?

You will need:

- your dark boxes
- a variety of lit light sources – torches, glow in the dark items, fairy lights, lamps, tablet screens, LED lights, glow sticks, etc.
- different coloured objects (not light sources)
- a variety of reflective objects – bike reflectors and high visibility clothing/cycle clips, plastic baubles, tinsel, foil, metal objects.

 Storify the science

Turn to the page in the book where the rabbit sees the two eyes 'shining' in the forest. Ask the children whether they have ever seen eyes like that. They may tell you that they have seen cats' eyes reflecting.

(Cats' eyes do indeed reflect light because they have a reflective layer, called a reflective tapetum, behind the retina. Light passes through the light sensitive cells on the way in, reflects off the reflective tapetum behind the retina and passes through the light sensitive cells again. This helps the cat to see in low light conditions. But don't tell them this yet!)

Ask the children whether the wolf's eyes are shining light out like a torch does. They will give you various answers. Accept them all without judgement.

Let them know that you are going to find out more about these 'shining' eyes.

Show them a torch and a piece of foil. Turn on the torch and shine it on the foil. Announce the torch and the foil are both shining. Put the torch in the dark box and ask the children what they think they will see inside the box. Accept all answers then ask a child to look inside. Elicit the torch is giving out light so we can see inside the box. Take out the torch!

Now, repeat this sequence with a piece of foil. Ask the same questions and put it in the dark box. The foil will not be visible in the box.

Come to the conclusion that shining is not a useful word as the foil and the torch are clearly different. Decide to come up with better words. Introduce the term 'light source' for objects that give out light such as the torch and 'reflective' for items that sparkle in the light, such as foil. You could draw the diagrams shown above to show the difference.

Ask the children to think about the sun and the moon. Only one is a light source. Let them discuss which one they think it is. Elicit that the sun gives out light (and makes the world light in daytime) but the moon just reflects the light that the sun produces.

Provide the children with a tray full of light sources and reflective materials/objects and some materials/ objects that are neither light sources nor reflective.

Set the challenge

Get a whiteboard or page ready to record your results.

You are going to find out which of these objects are light sources and which are not.

Before you test each item, look at it carefully and decide whether you think it is a light source or a reflective material. This is your prediction. Record your prediction.

Once you have made a prediction, put that item in the dark box and look inside. Record whether you can see the object or not.

Did you get any surprising results?

Can you name some light sources?

Can you name some reflective materials/objects?

Were there any materials/objects that were neither a light source nor reflective?

Return to the book

Flick back to the page where the wolf's eyes are 'shining' in the forest.

Show the children a torch and a reflective object. Ask them whether they think the wolf's eyes are shining out light because they are a light source like the torch or whether they are reflective like the object you are holding.

Discuss whether we can shine light out of our eyes! Think back to the diagrams drawn last week of the light rays going into (not out of) our eyes. Elicit the wolf's eyes cannot shine light out of them. They must be reflective so there must be some light in the forest or we wouldn't be able to see the eyes.

Now would be a good time to return to cats' eyes and talk about the reflective layer behind the retina (see above).

Rewrite the sentence in the book so that it no longer uses the word 'shining' but uses the more accurate term 'reflecting' instead.

 ## Teacher's top tips

The main skills being used here are predicting, testing and recording in a table, so use the lesson to highlight why tables are useful in science. You could let the children record in their own way. Once you have finished you can look at the way they recorded their results. Some of them will be more organised than others. Pick out a few and discuss their relative merits. Then suggest they use a table to show their work and copy their results in an orderly fashion into a table in their books, e.g.:

Object/material	Prediction Will I be able to see it in the dark?	Test Can I see it in the dark?	Is it a light source?
torch			
mirror			
glowstick			

What results should I expect?

Only the light sources will be visible in the dark boxes.

 ## What next?

If you want to record your findings in a creative way then you could:

- Use the internet to find pictures of light sources and reflective objects. Cut them out and stick them into your books in two clear groups.

- Draw a big picture of the rabbit and his environment. Include some reflective items such as the pond and the moon. Include some light sources such as a car headlight or the light in a house. Mark all the light sources with an S. Mark the reflective materials with an R.

- Role-play: being a pair of rabbits looking at the moon. Discuss whether it is a light source or not. Can you explain why it is so bright in the sky?°

- Role-play: being a pair of rabbits arguing about the wolf's eyes. One thinks they are a light source. The other can explain what is really going on.

- Design an outfit to stop baby rabbits being run over in the dark. Explain whether your design uses light sources or reflective materials or both.

 ## Assessing children's understanding

The following statements are indicators of basic understanding:

- A torch is a light source

- The foil is reflective.

More advanced understanding:

- You can't see the foil in the dark box because it is not giving out light and without light we cannot see.

————————————

DARK SHADOWS

Story link
The rabbit is scared of his own shadow.

THE SCIENCE: Shadows

A shadow is formed when light is blocked by a material that light cannot pass through. We call these materials opaque. Our bodies are opaque so they will create a dark shadow in direct light.

In our daily lives, light comes from many different directions, casting shadows in many directions. As I write, I can see four shadows of my hand on the table as there are four spotlights in the ceiling above me. Each one is creating a shadow. There is also sunlight coming in through the window so my hand shadows are not very dark as the sunlight is lighting up the table below my hand. All these lights make it hard to understand what is going on.

The simplest way to experience shadows is when there is only one strong light source such as when we are outside and the sun is out.

When the sun is out, light comes directly from the sun. If the sun is to our left, a shadow will be cast to our right. It's nice and simple. So a sunny playground is a good place to start talking about shadows.

Children often ask where their shadows go when the sun goes in. The world is still lit by the sun so where have the shadows gone? When clouds cover the sun, they 'spread the light out' so that it is coming from all directions. The light still casts shadows but in the areas where those shadows would fall there is light from another direction. So we don't see any shadows.

If you want to create shadows in the classroom, you'll need to find a place where you can set up a nice strong light from one direction and not get too much light from other sources so that the shadows created by your strong light are clear.

Some materials do not create a dark shadow. This is because some light passes through them. If you look through a plastic bottle you'll be able to see through it. If you can see through it, then light must be passing through it into your eyes. We call these materials transparent. Their shadows are often very pale.

Some materials let some light through but you can't see details through it. Frosted glass and tissue paper will let some light through. You'd be able to see the light of the sun or a light bulb through the material but you wouldn't be able to see any details. We call these materials translucent. Their shadows will not be as dark as those made by an opaque material.

Investigation: What is the best material for a shadow puppet?

You will need:

- torches – one between two
- a variety of materials to test including opaque, transparent and translucent materials and some with holes. You could include: card, paper, wood, stone, foil, fabrics, bubblewrap, clear plastic wrappers, plastic bottles (incl. coloured ones), coloured cellophane wrappers, plastic wallets, plastic milk bottles, tissue paper, shower curtain fabric, netting and hessian
- white wall or A3 paper
- sheet, string and pegs to make a screen
- strong light source (I use the white board projector to project a blank document)
- lolly sticks or strong straws.

 # Storify the science

Re-read the first two pages of the book, where the rabbit first sees his shadow on the rock.

Ask the children about their own shadows. Discuss the places where they have noticed their shadows and find out how much they understand about how those shadows are formed.

On a sunny day, take the whole group into the playground and line them up with their backs to the sun so they can see you and their own shadow. Ask the following questions:

- Where is your shadow?
- Where is the sun?
- If you turn around, does the shadow go to the other side of you? Why not? (The sun hasn't moved.)
- Can you see your nose appear in the shadow? How did you make it appear? (Turn sideways!)
- Your shadow touches your feet. How can you make a gap between your shadow and your feet? (Jump!)
- Why do you think there is a shadow?

N.B. If it is not sunny, you could dim the overhead lights and use the strong light to demonstrate most of this in the classroom.

Return to the book

Note that the artist has accurately drawn the shadow connected to the feet of the rabbit, just like ours outside.

Flick to the page in the woods. The rabbit can't see his shadow there. Elicit that this is because there is no strong sunlight. It is shady. The trees have already blocked out the sunlight and made shadows.

Ask the children how the rabbit could make a shadow in the woods. Elicit that he could go to a sunny spot where there are no trees or maybe take a torch. He needs a light source, an opaque object and a screen.

Introduce the idea that we could use the light source and screen to make a shadow puppet theatre to act out the story of the rabbit. Set up the screen or show a short video of shadow puppets – there are lots on the internet.

Suggest that the children make some puppets. But which material would make the darkest shadow?

Use a torch to make a shadow with a clear plastic bottle. Look at the shadow when it falls on a white background and then on a dark background so the children can see they need to cast shadows on white to be able to see them clearly. Ask the children whether they think it makes a good shadow. Then hold up some foil. Notice that the shadows are quite different. Ask the children why that might be. Accept all answers.

Introduce the words transparent (like the plastic bottle), opaque (like the foil) and translucent (like tissue). Discuss the meaning of each word and how much light can get through each type of material.

 ## Set the challenge

You are going to test all of these materials to see which one makes the best shadow so you can choose a suitable material when you make your puppet.

When you test the materials think about:

- what you will do;
- which materials you will test;
- what you will look for;
- how you will know which is the darkest shadow;
- how you will make the test fair.

Make sure you write down the names of the materials that make the darkest shadows. Then decide which of these you will use to make a shadow puppet.

Also write down anything you observed that is interesting.

Teacher's top tips

Let the children work out how to do their own test. You can always stop the class and draw attention to children who are doing something sensible such as:

- forming the shadow on a plain white background;
- holding the material at same distance from the torch and screen;
- comparing two at the same time;
- recording their observations in an orderly way
- recording in a table.

If their recording ends up in a muddle, demonstrate how to draw a table and let them reorganise it into a table. Children will start using a table once they see that it helps them to look back at their recording and know what it means.

Turn all the classroom lights off and pull down the blinds!

Discuss the shadows they made. They are often excited by the coloured shadows. When you make puppets, you could poke holes for details such as eyes and cover the holes with the coloured cellophane to give the puppet coloured details, or use buttons.

You are going to use the puppets next week and ideally they need to be about 10 cm tall for this activity. Larger puppets may prove difficult to use.

 ## Finale

Draw a diagram of how a shadow is made. Show how the light rays that hit the object stop at that point while the light rays around the object continue to the ground or other surface.

Decide on the material that makes the darkest shadow and is suitable for making puppets. You will probably decide thickish card that is easily cut or foil that can be moulded into shape will make the best puppets.

Demonstrate how to make a puppet and mount it on a lolly stick as a handle.

Give the children time and materials to make a shadow puppet from the story. They could make a wolf, a rabbit or a tree. They could also make fish to go in the water. Let them use their imaginations.

Then let them perform the story. Do warn them not to look directly into the strong light.

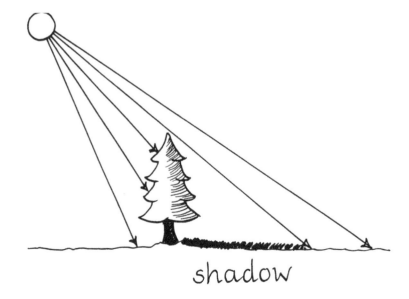

shadow

What results should I expect?

The opaque materials will make the darkest shadows but only some of them will be suitable for puppet making as some may be too floppy. The opaque materials with a very loose weave such as hessian or net may let light through the holes so the shadow will have light patches.

The transparent materials will make very pale shadows with dark spots where the plastic is not clear because it has been damaged.

The coloured cellophane and plastic will make coloured shadows.

The translucent materials will make grey shadows.

 ## What next?

If you want to record your findings in a creative way then you could:

- Write a script and perform your play. Make a video of your shadow puppet performance. Include a 'Behind the scenes' section at the end to show how the shadows are made.
- Write instructions about how to make a shadow puppet.
- Write another story about a group of naughty bunnies that terrorise baby wolves with shadow puppets of scary monsters. Maybe the naughty bunnies could get caught out when their torch runs out at a bad moment . . .

 ## Assessing children's understanding

The following statement is an indicator of basic understanding:

- If you block the light you make a shadow.

More advanced understanding:

- Blocking the light stops it from landing on the surface so a shadow forms in the place where the light rays can't reach.
- If some of the light can pass through an object placed in the path of the light then the shadow will be paler.

Patterns they may be able to describe:

- The more transparent the material, the paler the shadow.
- If the transparent material is coloured then the shadow is coloured in the same way.

THE ENORMOUS BLACK RABBIT

Story link
The rabbit's shadow frightens the wolf.

THE SCIENCE: How the size of a shadow changes

The way shadows change in size is best explained in diagrams. There are two things you can move when you cast a shadow on a screen: the light source and the object making the shadow.

Moving the light source

If the object is placed at a fixed distance to the screen and the light source is moved then the closer the light source is to the object, the larger the shadow will be. The largest shadow will be produced when the light source is right next to the object.

Moving the object

The further the object is from the light source, the smaller the shadow. The smallest the shadow can be is the size of the object itself and that will happen when the object is right next to the screen. The largest shadow will be produced by putting the object right next to the light source.

The edges of the shadow will be less distinct the further the light is from the object. This makes a difference to the clarity of a puppet's shadow and will be worth noting and discussing. We will be investigating moving the object rather than the light source.

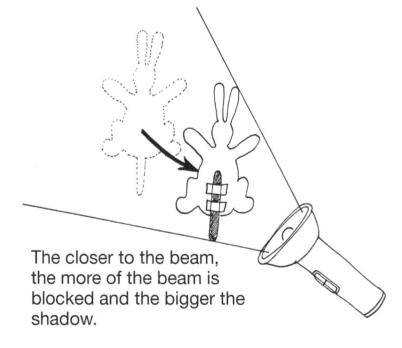

The closer to the beam, the more of the beam is blocked and the bigger the shadow.

INVESTIGATION: How do you make an enormous shadow?

You will need:

- torches (one between two)
- metre rulers
- 30 cm rulers
- large sheets of paper to create a screen

- a room where you can shut the blinds effectively
- sheet, string and pegs to make a screen
- strong light source (I use the white board projector to project a blank document).

 Storify the science

Re-read the part of the story where the rabbit is expecting the wolf to attack but he doesn't. Look at the artwork. How is the rabbit feeling when he 'shut his eyes tight but nothing happened'? How is the wolf feeling at that point? What can the wolf see?

Draw their attention to the huge shadow. Give out the shadow puppets you made last week and set up the screen and make torches available. Ask the children to go and work out how to make a huge shadow like the rabbit did. Give them time to play, to fiddle about with it, to tinker!

When you can see they have had some success at changing the size of the shadow, bring them back to the carpet and discuss what they found.

Listen to all their ideas. Ask if anyone measured how big their biggest shadow was. When you find no one has measured it, explain that when scientists start to notice something they take measurements so they can see whether there is a pattern.

This activity is all about pattern spotting and collecting accurate results so giving the children a pre-drawn table will help them to take the right measurements to spot the pattern. They'll need one like the table shown on the next page.

 Set the challenge

You are going to measure how big the shadow of your puppet is. This will work best with smaller puppets that are about 10 cm tall.

Set up the equipment as shown in the diagram on the next page.

Put paper on the wall where the light of the torch falls so you can write on it without damaging the wall!

Start by putting your puppet at the 10 cm mark on the ruler and mark the top and the bottom of the shadow (on your paper).

Record the height of the shadow in your table.

Now move the puppet to the 20 cm marker on the ruler and measure the shadow height again. Keep going until the shadow is right next to the wall.

Look at your results.

Could the shadow be 0 cm tall? Why? Could the shadow be 100m tall? How would you make that happen?

Can you see a pattern? If so, describe the pattern you can see.

Distance from light source (cm)	Height of shadow (cm)
10	
20	

 ## Teacher's top tips

This session is all about accuracy so encourage the children to find a way to keep the torch in a fixed position.

If you don't have enough wall space for children to work on, turn the desks on their sides to provide extra horizontal surfaces (as long as you feel it is safe).

You may find you need to have more than 1m between torch and wall in order to fit the shadow on your sheets of paper so try out the equipment before the lesson and ensure that what you are asking them to do with their puppets is actually possible!

They will notice that the shadow is sharper around the edges as the puppet moves closer to the wall. Discuss this and the implications for shadow puppet performances – the puppets must be close to the screen, which is tricky when there are too many puppeteers!

Discuss the pattern in the results and encourage the children to form sentences to describe the pattern that use two comparative words, e.g. bigger, taller, closer, further, smaller. The closer the puppet is to the wall, the smaller the shadow will be.

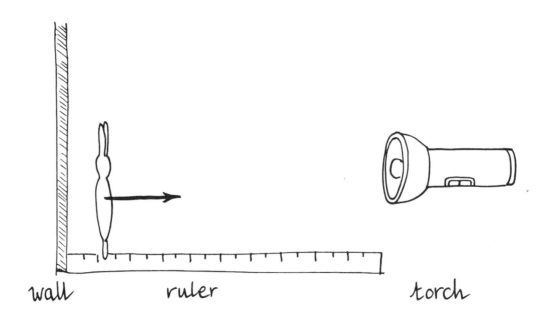

Draw diagrams to show how the beam of light spreads out from the source so blocking the light closer to the source blocks more of the beam, making a larger shadow.

What results should I expect?

The closer you move the puppet to the torch, the larger the shadow will be.

What next?

If you want to record your findings in a creative way then you could:

- Draw a line graph of your results. What shape is the graph? Can you use it to talk about how big the shadow could possibly be and how small it could possibly be?
- Write a letter to the rabbit with instructions for the rabbit about how to make a huge shadow in the forest, with a torch, to scare the wolf.
- Role-play: being Mummy Wolf explain to Daddy Wolf about shadows and how the shadow of a tiny rabbit can be so enormous.
- Write a diary entry for the rabbit about the day he met the wolf but his enormous black rabbit shadow scared it away. Make sure you explain why the shadow was so big.
- Write an advert for rabbits, selling your super wolf-repelling torch. Explain how your torch can be used to scare wolves.
- Write a scientific report for the newspaper recounting the events in the book and explaining the science behind the enormous rabbit shadow.

Assessing children's understanding

The following statement is an indicator of basic understanding:

- A shadow puppet can make shadows of different sizes, depending where you put it.

More advanced understanding:

- The beam of light spreads out from the source. So, the beam is smaller, closer to the light source. Therefore the closer the puppet is to the source, the more light is blocked so the larger the shadow.

Patterns they may be able to describe:

- The closer the puppet is to the light source the bigger the shadow.

TOO BRIGHT?

Story link
It is a bright sunny day.

THE SCIENCE: Blocking harmful light

Too much light can be very harmful for our eyes. On a bright sunny day we may feel the need to squint or even close our eyes to shut out some of the light. Our retina is very delicate and too much light can destroy the sensitive cells. For this reason, our eyes have a clever shutter system. The coloured part of our eye (the iris) is a muscle that can contract and reduce the size of the pupil when the light levels are high. When the light levels are low this muscle can relax and the pupil is expanded to let in more light. When we move from low light levels to high (or the reverse) it takes our eyes and brain a moment to readjust so that we can see properly.

Looking directly at a strong light can damage our eyes. Even with our pupils contracted, light still enters the eye and if this light is very strong, it can damage the retina. Looking directly at the sun can cause damage, which is why special glasses are essential during an eclipse, when the temptation to stare at the sun can be irresistible.

Sunlight is made up of many different colours of light. Our eyes can only detect some of them. The ones we can see are present in a natural rainbow. There are other forms of light that our eyes cannot detect because they are outside the range sensed by our retinas. One of these is UV light which is harmful to our skin and our eyes. When we choose sunglasses we should make sure that they have been made to block out this harmful light.

INVESTIGATION: Looking after our eyes

You will need:

- UV colour changing beads (the ones that go pink or purple) available online
- red and yellow coloured cellophane
- clingfilm
- other transparent plastics
- small shallow pots/petri dishes.

Storify the science

Flick quickly through the book and stop at a few different pages, asking the children how bright the light is in that scene. Ask the children to think about a recent sunny day. How does it affect our eyes when we come in from a bright sunny day into a darker space or when you open the curtains in a dark room to find it is sunny outside? Share stories of how it takes our eyes a while to adjust.

Tell the children that too much light damages our eyes. Looking directly at the sun or at a bright torch can be harmful. Don't rush this part – they need to remember it.

Explain that our eyes have a safety device built in! Without explaining further, ask them to get into pairs. Have one of each pair close their eyes and count to 50. While their partner watches closely, ask the child to open their eyes. It should be possible to see the pupil contract as they go from darkness into light.

You might need to let the children have a few goes. They don't always catch it the first time.

The next set of activities are based on the Royal Society of Chemistry's project called 'Mission Starlight' which you might want to look up on their website. It is full of useful resources. Thank you to the RSC for their permission to use their ideas here. It uses UV colour changing beads which are safe as long as they are not a choking hazard so warn children not to put them in their mouths. They change colour when exposed to UV. The more UV light, the darker the colour they go. The RSC recommends using only the ones that go pink and purple.

Introduce the idea of UV light to the children. They might have heard of it from suncream adverts or experienced it at a disco. Let them know it is bad for their skin and for their eyes.

 # Set the challenge

You are going to find out which material is best for blocking out UV light so that we can find out which might be best for making the rabbit some sunglasses for very bright days.

You will be given some UV colour changing beads. Take one outside into the sunlight and watch what happens. Bring it inside again and watch what happens. Why is it different outside?

Your task is to find out which material blocks the most UV light.

When you design your test think about:

*   how to set up your test;
*   how long you will leave the beads in the sunlight;
*   which materials you will test;
*   what you will look for (how you will know if something has changed);
*   ways to make sure the light goes through the material you are testing and not around the edges;

- how you will make your test fair;
- how you will record your results.

Which material did you find to be the best at blocking out the UV?

Use that material to make a pair of sunglasses for the rabbit.

 ## Teacher's top tips

Let the children have time to plan what they want to do. You could then agree a basic method, before beginning, if you think they need guidance about making the test fair as you do want to try to get some valid results.

Make sure you make tiny sets of glasses, too small to be worn by the children so that they don't try to wander around the classroom wearing something that is not appropriate human eye wear!

You could cut out mini card sunglasses like the old cardboard 3D glasses so the children can easily stick the material into the holes you have cut. Or you can let the children make their own from card and straws or pipe cleaners. Again, do make sure they make them rabbit sized!

You can print out colour charts from the RSC website that help to identify the level of colour change.

What results should I expect?

It depends on the materials you have available to test. You should find that some allow the beads to change colour more than the others. The bead that changes colour least will be under the material that blocks the most UV.

 ## What next?

If you want to record your findings in a creative way then you could:

- Find out which fabrics block the most UV light and recommend these as school uniform options in the summer.
- Design the packaging for the rabbit sunglasses. Include a leaflet explaining how to look after our eyes.
- Role-play: being an optician. Persuade the rabbit that he should buy your glasses.
- Write an advert to go in a health magazine advertising the benefits of wearing your glasses.
- Role-play: being a science presenter on a TV show, explain how the materials for your glasses were tested.

Assessing children's understanding

The following statement is an indicator of basic understanding:

- The beads changed colour in the sunlight.

More advanced understanding:

- The sunlight contains UV light which makes the beads change colour.
- You can't see the UV light.
- UV light is bad for our skin and our eyes.

Patterns they may be able to describe:

- The more UV that reaches the beads, the darker colour they go.

_____

3 *The Last Wild*

Piers Torday (2013)

TOPIC PLANNER

Story link	Science: Food chains, microbes, digestion, teeth	Activity	Page
The varmints	Classification Biological keys	Grouping objects (activity) Making keys (activity)	35–6
Weasels or badgers?	Biological keys	Using keys Identifying local wildlife – go outside! (activity)	41
Natural order	Food chains and food webs – the effect of environmental change on animals Drawing food chains	Making food chains (activity)	44
Exterminate them	Microbes Disease spreading Designing a fair test Changing one variable	Microbes – nasty or nice? Glitter-hand (demo) Growing microbes part 1 (yeast) (investigation) Growing microbes part 2 (bread mould) (investigation) Wash your hands! (activity)	50–1

Story link	Science:	Activity	Page
Red-eye	Population dynamics and wildlife management Modelling population change	Grass, rabbits and foxes (activity)	57–8
Feast	Digestion Modelling digestion	Modelling the gut! (activity) This activity requires you to make a piece of equipment with basic household objects	64–5
A trial drug	Teeth Mouse, wolf, human, deer Also pigeon and cockroach Vaccines Designing an object to solve a problem	Design a route for Laura II (research and design activity) Edward Jenner (research)	69

THE VARMINTS

Story link

All of the animals in the world have been killed by the virus apart from the useless ones – 'the varmints'.

THE SCIENCE 1: Classification (grouping organisms by their features)

The idea that one species could evolve into another is a relatively new idea. In the past, people had always considered animals as fixed and unchanging in their form. They attempted to group things together but came up with some very odd groups. Cotton and wool are similar but one comes from a plant and one from an animal. As they seemed similar materials, stories grew that linked the origins of these two together. This seems ridiculous now, in the light of our understanding of the theory of evolution and Linnaeus' systematic classification.

Linnaeus (1707–1778) was a Swedish botanist who was determined to find a way to systematically name plants so that plants with similar features could be grouped together. He improved upon the ideas of other botanists who came before him and grouped and named all the plants and animals, that had been identified at the time, according to his binomial (two name – genus/species) system. He used the physical features of the plants and animals (e.g. seed type) to put them into sensible groups.

Classification helps scientists to organise the huge array of living things into groups. These groups reflect their evolutionary history too as one species can evolve into another closely related species. Once organised, the differences between different species or different groups are easier to observe.

When grouping living things, we need to look closely at important features that distinguish one organism from another. Both a moth and a cheetah can be spotty but this doesn't put the two animals into the same group. The number of legs is important, as is the way it reproduces and whether it has warm blood.

N.B. Children often choose groupings that are illogical, e.g. spotty/four-legged/has wings. They need to know that groupings have to answer **one** question at a time, e.g. How many legs? 2 legs/4 legs/6 legs/8 legs/many legs.

ACTIVITY 1: Grouping objects

You will need:

- a large selection of one type of object – enough for five per pair/group of children. (I use shoes because I have lots! You might choose cups or pens. You need objects that are essentially the same thing but have many different patterns, shapes or features. You could use photos of objects.)

- a photograph of a cockroach, a moth and a spider.

 ## Storify the science

Read the first few pages of the book to the children. Stop when you reach the end of the part where Kester is standing in line for his lunch (p. 10). Draw a circle on the board and label it 'varmints'. Write all the animals that Kester mentions in the circle: moths, spiders, cockroaches.

These are the animals that have survived the 'red-eye'. Ask what these animals have in common and what distinguishes them from one another. Ask whether the children think they all belong in one group. In what ways are they similar or different? Ask them what features they might consider in order to decide.

 ## Set the challenge

You are going to decide how to group the objects I am going to give you. You can choose the groups but you must be able to explain why you put something in that group.

Name each group you have chosen and be ready to share those group names with the class.

You will be asked to swap your objects and repeat this activity a few times.

 ## Teacher's top tips

The point of this activity is to help the children, by trial and error, to learn to sort objects into sensible groups based on one feature alone, e.g. colour OR pattern. Let the children sort the objects and then share their groups with you. Find children who have chosen sensible groupings based on one feature and explain why those make sense.

Listen out for the following errors:

- nonsensical grouping, e.g. blue shoes/high heels/boots. This grouping involves both colour and form;

- groupings that are subjective and hence won't be agreed upon by all, e.g. nice shoes and horrible shoes;

- groupings that are not obvious by looking at the object itself, e.g. this one is kept in a box, this one is kept on a shelf.

Gently encourage them to stick to one obvious visible physical feature at a time, instead.

Repeat the process a few times to make sure every child can accurately group the objects according to physical features. Keep swapping the objects so that there's a new challenge each time.

Move fast. Give them two minutes maximum each time. They don't need long!

What results should I expect?

Ideally, all the children should be able to suggest sensible groups based on one physical feature, e.g. 2 buttons/4 buttons/no buttons OR blue/not blue.

 THE SCIENCE 2: Biological keys

A biological key is used to identify a particular animal or plant by answering a series of questions that only have two answers. Usually the answer is yes or no:

Does the animal have fur? Yes/No

Sometimes a question must be phrased to give a yes/no answer, e.g. the question 'How many legs/arms does it have?' could have the answer none, two, four, six, eight or many. In order to have only two possible answers, this question would need rephrasing into:

- Does it have eight legs? Yes/No

 ACTIVITY 2: Making keys

You will need:

- a selection of biological keys (you could write your own to fit a set of sweets);
- a set of pictures of imaginary animals (I use Flanimal pictures (by Rob Steen) from the internet) or real animals or plants. You must be able to see details such as number of legs, in the pictures, which is why the cartoon animals I use work so well. Besides, monsters are fun!

 Storify the science

Return to the group of varmints listed on the board. Ask the children whether they can put the animals in the varmint group into two groups. Show them photos of these animals and let them count legs and discuss what kind of creatures they are. Lead them into the grouping of insects (moth and cockroach) and spiders.

Introduce Linnaeus as a scientist who looked at the features of plants and animals and grouped them accordingly. There are lots of videos on the internet about Linnaeus and his classification system so find one that will suit your class and use it to introduce the main points about his life and work in classification.

Ask the children to imagine they had been locked up all their life, like Kester, and had never seen a live animal (except the varmints). Imagine going out into the school grounds/local park/ forest. They might find a worm and think it was a snake. They might find a bluebird and think it was an eagle. Help the children to understand that Linnaeus' way of grouping animals helps us to organise the huge array of living things and helps us to compare similar animals to find important differences between them. It also helps us to identify animals we don't recognise.

Show the children a pre-written key. Introduce the way a key works using yes/no questions to get to an answer. You may want to use sweets or whatever your children are keen on, to get their attention! Spend a little time trying out these keys, getting the hang of answering one question and moving down the correct branch of the tree to the next question.

Explain that keys help us to sort animals into the correct groups and identify them.

Remind the children of their work earlier, grouping the object according to one physical feature at a time.

Show them four imaginary animals and demonstrate how to ask yes/no questions to create the key.

It might look like the sorting branch diagram on the facing page.

 ## Set the challenge

You are going to make a key that can differentiate between four animals/plants. You will need to ask some yes/no questions in your key.

Practise your key on scrap paper then ask your teacher to check it works, before you make your best copy.

Look closely at your animals. Choose yes/no questions that are easy to answer from the pictures you have. You should be able to answer the question you chose, easily.

 ## Teacher's top tips

The best way to understand how something works is to have a go, yourself, so making keys is a great way to understand how they work and using imaginary animals makes it fun.

Practise the key on scrap paper before putting it into their books. It is hard to get it right first time.

Make sure you check each key works – children have a tendency to try each question out on every animal, even if it has been eliminated from that branch of the key. To help them with this, encourage the children to move each picture of the animal down the lines of the key to its destination and then leave it there, while they sort the rest.

What results should I expect?

Ideally, all the children should be able to suggest sensible groups based on one physical feature and draw a key that will separate the four creatures they were given.

 ## What next?

If you want to record your findings in a creative way then you could:

- Write instructions for Kester about how to use your key.
- Make a poster that you might find at Spectrum Hall, warning children to stay away from animals, including a key, that would identify the varmints Kester talks about.
- Write a book of 'Lost Wildlife' about the wildlife you think Kester might have encountered on his island. They could be real animals or imaginary ones. Draw and name your creatures and write a brief description of each. Then, design a key that would identify these animals.

 ## Assessing children's understanding

The following statements are indicators of basic understanding:

- Keys help you to identify an animal or plant.
- Keys ask questions about physical features of the animal or plant.
- The questions must have only two possible answers.
- Organising animals into groups based on their physical characteristics helps scientists to compare animals and identify them.

More advanced understanding:

- The child can create a key that accurately identifies a set of animals or plants by writing sensible questions with only two possible answers. (The more animals or plants you include in the key, the more questions will be required to separate them into groups and identify them.)

WEASELS OR BADGERS

Story link

Kester has never seen the creatures before and cannot identify them accurately.

THE SCIENCE: Biological keys

You'll find everything you need to know about biological keys earlier in this chapter on p. 37.

ACTIVITY: Using keys

You will need:

- biological keys of the animals and plants in your local area
- biological key apps on iPads if possible
- mini-beast collecting equipment (nets, white sheets and pooters)
- pots/tanks to put mini-beasts in
- magnifying glasses
- camera to record animals collected, if required
- sensible clothing
- plenty of adult help.

Storify the science

Read the second part of the book up to p. 69, where Kester notices the animals have red eyes. Ask the children why Kester didn't recognise all the animals correctly. Ask the children whether they think it matters if he doesn't know the names of the animals. Listen to all their opinions and ask them to justify their answers. Lead them to the idea that we, as humans, cannot look after our environment if we don't know what is out there. How can we notice a change if we have no idea what our environment should look like?

Talk to them about the phrase 'Spring is early this year!' People often say it. Ask the children what they think this means. Lead them to the idea that people notice flowers blooming earlier than usual and that we only know it is early if we take notice of when they usually bloom.

Changing weather patterns can affect the living organisms. Scientists make records and notice changes.

Ask the children whether there are any changes made by humans in their local area: are there new buildings or new roads? Ask whether they have noticed changes in the wildlife as a result.

If we are going to be good custodians of the Earth we must get to know the place where we live.

 # Set the challenge

You are going to find out what animals and plants live in your local area. Be on the lookout for species that are under threat, such as the Horse Chestnut which is under threat from leaf miners.

Try to learn the names of the trees that grow in or near your school grounds.

Try to find out which animals are there too.

Use the magnifying glasses to look closely at the physical features.

Remember, catch mini-beasts carefully and put them back where you found them once you've identified them.

Use keys of all types to help you, as well as identification charts.

 # Teacher's top tips

This is an ideal activity for a trip out to an outdoor centre where they can provide pond dipping or you could do this as part of Forest Schools. You can always link it to the story before you go. However, you are likely to have a few trees in your school grounds and it is worth getting to know these too.

The more adults you can recruit, the better. Catching mini-beasts can be fiddly and needs to be done carefully. Going outdoors can also be very distracting for the over excitable child so extra adults to keep minds focussed will make the time more productive.

Take some time to get to know your local trees and plants so you can help the children learn and keep them safe if any plants shouldn't be handled. A good website for reference and identification materials is The Woodland Trust.

Find out if you have any rare species living in your area and encourage children to get to know and learn how to protect them. In my local area, there are Great Crested Newts so we study the way these are surveyed and their population is tracked so that any changes can be noted and the causes investigated. Local conservation groups are usually happy to come in and speak to children about the area in which they live.

What next?

If you want to record your findings in a creative way then you could:

- Use your knowledge of local trees and mini-beasts to write an alternative chapter where Kester arrives in the place that you and your class have explored. Include moments where Kester mistakes one animal for another and has to be corrected by The General. Try to describe the animals and plants with a sense of awe and wonder as you meet each one. Illustrate your story with some detailed drawings of the things you have described.

- Make a logbook of plants, trees, insects, arachnids and other invertebrates that you found. If you are lucky enough to find vertebrate animals, include them too. Draw and name each one and give a brief description so that someone else, using your logbook, could identify them too.

- Make your own key to identify the trees in your school grounds. Use features such as tree shape, appearance and bark as well as leaf shape and flowers. Share these keys with another class.

- Design a home for a species that needs looking after in your area. You could even make bird feeders and hang them up in school to encourage local bird species. Remember to avoid using nuts, as children may have allergies, and to find out which seeds will encourage which bird species. Then hang it in a place where you can see the birds feeding but where droppings won't hinder playtime.

Assessing children's understanding

The following statement is an indicator of basic understanding:

- The children can identify some local trees and animals.

More advanced understanding:

- The children can make their own keys using leaf shape etc. to identify local trees.

———————————————

NATURAL ORDER

Story link

The wolves insist that the natural order must be maintained.

THE SCIENCE: Food chains and food webs

Animals and plant species that live in a particular place are reliant upon one another. Sometimes this is an obvious relationship, e.g. the owl eats the mice in the cornfield. Sometimes the relationship is less obvious, e.g. the seed is more likely to germinate if it has passed through the gut of a bird. Any interdependent species are part of the same ecosystem.

Food chains are just one way in which species are linked. The energy from the sun is captured by plants and made into plant materials such as cellulose and sugars that cause the plant to grow. These plants are called producers. This energy passes to consumers when herbivores eat the plants and then to carnivores when the herbivore is eaten. A food chain diagram shows the flow of this energy up the food chain.

A consumer cannot make their own food. They eat other organisms to get their energy.

ACTIVITY: Making food chains

You will need:

- enlarged copies of the silhouettes overleaf. (If you like, you could cut holes for the eyes and put red acetate behind and display on the window so that their eyes glow red.)
- copies of the food chain cards pre-cut into single cards (and laminated, if you prefer). You'll need one per child.
- copies of the entire food chain card sheet (uncut) – one per child.

Storify the science

Have the enlarged silhouettes of the animals cut out and stuck to a window or display board that you can reach from where you will teach. Make sure you can write on the window with a dry-wipe pen or on the backing paper if you are working on a display board.

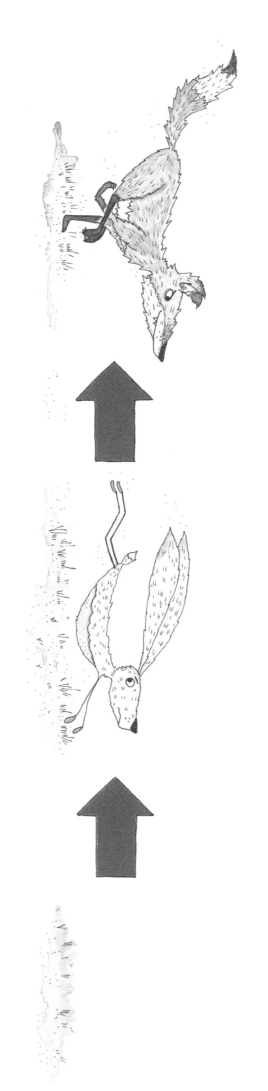

Re-read Part 2 to the point where all the animals have emerged and the wolves have insisted that the natural order must be maintained (p. 80).

Ask the children what they understand by the term 'natural order'. Lead them to the idea that one animal eats another and that the wolf is top of the food chain – nothing eats the wolf. In this book, the wolf is also seen as the leader because he is at the top of the food chain. You may like to discuss how the term 'natural order' can be seen in terms of leadership but, in biological terms, it merely means the order of the food chain.

Ask the children what the wolf might eat. Wolves tend to hunt in packs and bring down large prey so the most likely prey animal in this selection is the deer. Draw a line between the wolf and the deer to show they are linked.

Give each child a pre-cut card showing animals you might find in the woodland mentioned in the book (overleaf). Ask them to read their card and then find someone holding a card that is linked to theirs, e.g. the earthworm is eaten by the badger so they are linked.

The children should find that they don't all end up in pairs. Some food chains have three links. Collect in the sets of linked cards and stick them to the white board. Start with the deer and wolf. Demonstrate how these can be made into a food chain such as the one shown below. Emphasise that the energy (or food) flows from the producer to the consumers and from herbivore to carnivore and that the arrow represents this flow.

Discuss how many apples a deer might eat in a year (maybe a quarter of the apples on a tree) and how many deer a wolf might eat (maybe 20) and therefore how many apple trees would be required to support one wolf (maybe five trees per wolf).

Ask which other food chain included the apple tree. Lead them to the idea that more than one food chain can be dependent on the apple tree. A drawing of all these linked food chains would be called a food web.

 ## Set the challenge

You are going to find out how the animals and plants in this 'Ring of Trees' are linked.

Use the information on the sheet of cards to draw as many food chains as you can. (See next page.)

Now cut the sheet into cards. Stick the plants in the middle of a clean piece of A3 paper and arrange the herbivores around them, near the plants that they eat. Then stick the carnivores down near the herbivores that they eat. Now draw lines from one animal to another to show they are linked. You should end up with a food web.

 ## Teacher's top tips

Once the children have worked out all the food links, discuss the complexity of their food web diagram and make a class version on the window or display board with the enlarged silhouettes.

Earthworm
I eat dead leaves

Grass

Golden Eagle
I eat badgers and hares

Apple Tree

Deer
I eat fruit grass and bark

Apple Tree

Hare
I eat grass and fruit

Badger
I eat earthworms and apples

Wolf   I eat deer and hares

What results should I expect?

The children can draw an accurate food chain with the arrows flowing in the right direction and understand that, in an ecosystem, there will be more than one food chain and all these chains will interlink to make a food web.

 Finale

Give out the pre-cut cards again. Give one to each child and stand them in a ring. Give one child a ball of string and ask them to hold the end. Keeping hold of this end, they must throw the ball of string to another child who has a card that is linked to their own (e.g. the apple tree is linked to the deer). This child keeps hold of their section of string and throws the remaining ball of string to someone holding another linked card. Continue until all the children are holding onto a part of the string and it is criss-crossing the space in the centre of the ring of children. Keep it taut.

Now choose a child, holding an animal, whose string is interwoven with many others. Declare that this animal has the red-eye and make him sit down. If this movement causes the string of another child to dip, they must also sit down. This should cause a ripple effect so that all children will end up sitting down.

Explain that there is a fine balance in nature – a natural order. When this is upset by humans or disease or a change in the environment, it may only initially affect one species but as all species are interconnected, all species in the ecosystem are eventually affected, and often in ways we cannot predict.

 What next?

If you want to record your findings in a creative way then you could:

* Make another food web using the animals and plants in your local habitat that you have been learning to identify in previous weeks.
* Role-play a conversation between the stag and Kester, where the stag explains how all the creatures are linked and there is a natural order to the food chains.
* Write a short booklet entitled 'The Natural Order'. You could write it from the point of view of the wolf as a top predator and explain how you need all the layers of the food chain to be in place so that you can eat. Also, explain how much plant matter is required to support all the herbivores that a wolf needs to eat.
* Investigate a species of animal that is under threat of extinction due to human activity. For example, our local badgers are affected by building houses and roads so you could engage your children in a debate with one half of the class, arguing the need for new houses and homes for humans while the other half argue the need for land for the badgers. One global issue you could research is the theory that global warming, due to human pollution, is shrinking the polar ice caps and putting polar bears at risk.

Assessing children's understanding

The following statements are indicators of basic understanding:

- You can make a food chain from: apple tree, deer, wolf.
- There is usually more than one food chain in an ecosystem.

More advanced understanding:

- Animals and plants in an ecosystem are linked in all kinds of ways so if something changes, e.g. one animal gets a disease, then all the animals in the ecosystem can be affected. The knock-on effects of one small change can be huge and hard to predict.

EXTERMINATE THEM

 Story link

Kester and Polly encounter Captain Skuldiss and the cullers.

 ## THE SCIENCE: Microbes

We are covered in microbes both inside and out: bacteria, viruses and fungi (which includes yeasts and moulds). Most of them cause us no harm and our bodies are accustomed and adapted to their presence. Indeed, many of them are essential for our bodies to function properly. We have bacteria in our gut that are essential for efficient digestion.

However, some microbes cause diseases. They can be spread from one person to another by coughing, sneezing. One person sneezes on their hands and then touches someone else and the microbes are passed on by the touch. These microbes (or germs) cannot live long outside the body of their host (us). They rely on the warmth, the moisture and the food provided by our bodies to survive so most will not last long on our skin or on dry household objects. Washing our hands before we touch our food and eat is a good precaution to stop most of these microbes from entering our bodies and making us sick.

Some microbes are important in food production, e.g. making bread, cheese, beer and wine. Yeast produces bubbles of carbon dioxide as it ferments, which gives the bubbles to bread and sparkling wines and beers. It also produces alcohol which remains in the beer but is evaporated out of bread by the heat in the cooking process. Mould gives the cheese its flavour. These microbes are harmless.

Another essential function of microbes is to recycle. Microbes are essential in the rotting process. They convert organic materials such as dead leaves and dead animals into useful nutrients that can be absorbed by plants and thus be part of living organisms again.

All microbes are living organisms. They need food, water, oxygen and warmth. Many are adapted to live in extreme environments but will still need these basic requirements in some form.

Scientists argue that viruses are not alive, based on this definition, as all they need to replicate is a host cell.

 ## DEMO AND INVESTIGATIONS: Microbes – nasty or nice?

You will need:

- glitter dust (very fine glitter powder – available from party shops)
- yeast (dried yeast for baking)
- balloons
- small pots – film canisters work well
- sugar
- warm water and cold water
- bread
- transparent plastic food bags
- UV torch
- gel or dust that will glow in the dark and is safe to use in the classroom (search online for glo germ powder).

 ## Storify the science

Before you begin, rub a little glitter dust onto the palm of your hand. Keep the palms of your hands out of sight of the children.

Read up to page 150 where Captain Skuldiss explains that he wants to exterminate all the diseased animals. Ask the children why they think he is trying to kill all the animals. Elicit that killing all the animals would get rid of the red-eye too.

Ask the children what the red-eye is and discuss the diseases they know of. Elicit that disease can be caused by microbes that are too small to see.

Now make a show of congratulating a child (Child A) who gave you a correct answer in your discussion. Shake their hand firmly and get them glittery without drawing attention to it. Then insist that they shake hands with some other children in the room who gave good answers – make a show of it and make sure they shake hands firmly. Then tell them they all did well and let them all shake hands with everyone around them. Let them carry on for a moment, even if they start moving around. You want the glitter spread as far as possible.

Now call the class back to attention. Tell them you have a disease. A very contagious disease called the glitter-hand. Ask them to check themselves for signs of infection. Discuss how easily the glitter was spread and how easily a disease such as the red-eye could spread.

Tell the children you are going to look at the pattern of the spread of infection in slow motion.

- Stand Child A at the front of the class.

- Imagine this child shook hands with two people and infected them. Stand two more children up in a row in front of Child A.

- Then these two children infected two more each. Stand four more children up in a new row.

- Predict how many rows/sets of handshakes it would take to infect the whole class.

- It should only take four rows of children (two, four, eight, 16). So, it doesn't take long to infect the whole class.

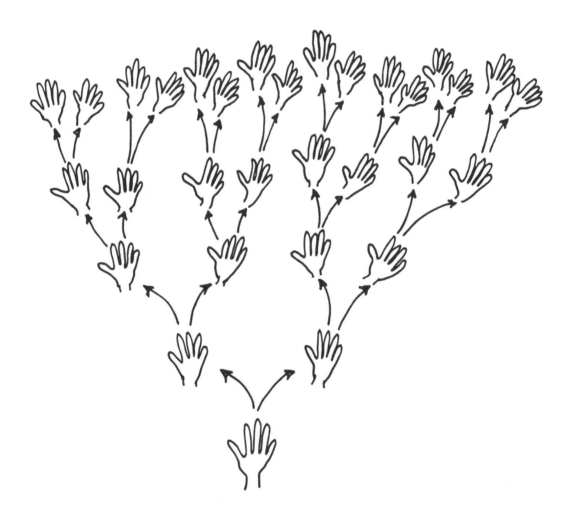

Explain that thankfully, the glitter-hand disease won't kill you. You shouldn't rub it in your eyes but it won't kill you. This is because glitter is not alive. (You may want to wash the glitter off at this point.)

Introduce the idea that the microbes that cause disease are alive. They grow in the bodies of other animals because they have oxygen, water, food and warmth.

Some microbes don't cause disease – they help us.

Set the challenge

Growing microbes part 1 (yeast)

You are going to investigate microbes to see what makes them grow fastest. You will be working with yeast we use to make bread, which is harmless to humans.

First, place a teaspoon of yeast into a little pot and add some warm water. Secure a balloon over the top and watch what happens.

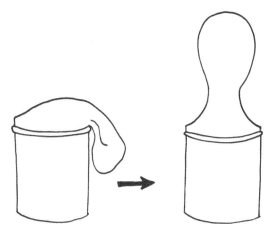

When the yeast starts to grow, it makes carbon dioxide bubbles. Can you tell whether your yeast is alive?

We know that microbes need food, oxygen, warmth and water to grow.

How could you prove this? Design a test to gather the evidence that the yeast grows fastest in certain conditions.

When you design your test think about:

- what you will change;
- how you will make sure only one variable is changed at a time;
- what you will measure;
- how you will measure it.

Hint – you can always compare it to the pot of yeast with warm water that you did at the start.

 ## Teacher's top tips

The balloon will expand as bubbles of carbon dioxide are produced. The quicker they grow, the quicker they fill the balloon with gas.

Let the children choose what to investigate. They could try any of the following:

- cold water vs warm water vs hot;
- sugar vs no sugar;
- water vs no water.

They could measure the time taken for the balloon to stand upright.

They could measure the circumference of the balloon at its widest (with string) after a certain length of time.

They could simply rank the balloons from fullest to emptiest.

The experimental design may not be perfect so allow them to refine their ideas as they go and if you want to record a method, write it retrospectively when they know what works. You learn more by getting it wrong first and solving the problem than by being told how to get it right.

What results should I expect?

The yeast will grow well in the warm, with plenty of sugar.

It won't grow without water.

It won't grow in very cold water. Very hot water will kill it.

Growing microbes part 2 (bread mould)

You are going to investigate microbes that would make us sick but are still extremely helpful to us as recyclers. As they make us sick, we will have to make sure we seal them in plastic so we don't touch the microbes themselves. We will be working with bread mould.

You will be given two slices of bread and two plastic bags.

Before you start, you are going decide what you could investigate about growing bread mould.

Put one slice of bread into a bag without making any changes.

Choose one variable to change on the other slice, which might affect mould growth – e.g. adding something to the bread. Then close up the bag, leaving a little gap so that air can get in and leave it for a week. We'll look at them again next week.

Think about:

- what might make the mould grow faster;
- what might make it grow slower;
- where you will leave the bread.

Remember, the mould breaks the bread down into nutrients that a plant could use so it recycles the bread into something useful for the plant. Imagine a world where the food we discard was not recycled in this way.

 ## Teacher's top tips

Let the children choose what to investigate. They could try any of the following:

- wet vs dry bread/toast;
- sugar vs no sugar;
- warm vs cold place.

IMPORTANT – Make sure the bags are not completely sealed. If air cannot get in, you will create anaerobic conditions in which some nasty microbes may thrive. Check each bag so make sure there is a small gap to let the air in.

Leave the bags mostly sealed in this way all week and don't open them when you observe them. Look at the bread through the bag.

Use magnifiers to observe the mould. If you have a hand-held digital microscope you can connect to the smart board. Viewing mould up close is fascinating.

Emphasise how important microbes are in decay and recycling of nutrients.

Again, the experimental design may not be perfect so allow them to refine their ideas as they go and if you want to record a method, write it retrospectively when they know what works.

Don't open the bags. Dispose of them immediately at the end of the lesson without opening.

What results should I expect?

The mould will grow well in the warm.

It won't grow without water.

It won't grow in the cold.

They may want to add sugar but the bread is food enough to make mould grow. However, if they are curious, let them try it. They'll see from others that the mould will grow on the bread without sugar.

 Finale

While the children are out of the classroom, put 'glo germ' powder (which glows under UV light) on your hands and go around the classroom touching doorhandles, desks, pencil cases, the whiteboard, pens etc. You may want to keep it on your hands. You may want to dust the hands of another adult in the room or even leave a trail to the head's office and ask them to join in the fun and dust their hands with the powder.

Pay special attention to the property of one child who you know is likely to play along once they realised they have been 'infected'. Coat their pencil case in the powder.

When the children come in, return to the story. Imagine being Kester and knowing that animals all around you could be infected with a deadly virus. The virus is microscopic – you wouldn't be able to see it. Until the animal got sick and developed red-eyes, you wouldn't be able to tell which animals were infected with the virus. Without knowing, the virus could spread from animal to animal.

Sometimes, scientists can work out where an infection started by looking at the way it spreads. Imagine that there is a mystery virus in the room. We have to work out where it started.

Get out the UV torch and shine it on a handprint that you made previously. Tell them it is a fake virus that can only be seen under UV light. Ask one child to search other places in the room for the virus and to work out which adult infected the room.

Discuss how microbes are easily spread by people touching each other and touching objects and furniture.

Seek out the child whose pencil case was coated in powder. Ask if you can check their hands. Hopefully the powder will be on them. Emphasise the importance of hand washing in the prevention of the spread of disease and demonstrate how to wash hands thoroughly, front and back. Send the children to wash and check for any leftover powder with the torch.

 ## What next?

If you want to record your findings in a creative way then you could:

* Write a leaflet or poster for the wall in Spectrum Hall warning about the spread of disease and the importance of washing your hands;
* Role-play: Polly explaining to Kester why the bag of dry cat biscuits hasn't gone mouldy;
* Use yeast to make bread. Write the recipe and explain why the yeast is vital in this process;
* Role-play: being a hygienist, demonstrating how to wash your hands properly.

 ## Assessing children's understanding

The following statements are indicators of basic understanding:

* Microbes are tiny living creatures.
* Some microbes can harm us by causing disease.
* Some microbes cause decay and help us by recycling dead plants and animals.
* Some microbes are needed to make food such as yeast in bread.
* Diseases can be spread by touching or coughing or sneezing so we should wash our hands before we touch our food.

More advanced understanding:

* The spread of disease can be very rapid as the numbers of infected people can double very easily.

RED-EYE

Story link

Ma explains how it was the farm animals that caught the red-eye first and then this had devastating knock-on effects.

THE SCIENCE: Population dynamics and wildlife management

When a small change occurs in the environment, this can lead to a huge change in the population of animals in that environment. When there is less rainfall, less grass grows and rabbits have less to eat. Starving rabbits cannot reproduce so fewer rabbits are born. Foxes eat rabbits so when the number of rabbits falls, more foxes will go hungry and, as they can't reproduce when malnourished, the population of foxes declines too.

Sometimes, small changes lead to unforeseen eventualities, e.g. the introduction of a few grey squirrels to the UK by the Victorians. It is likely that the Victorians had no idea that this would upset the population of red squirrels as much as it did. Research suggests that the effect was threefold. First, the grey squirrels introduced a disease (squirrel pox) that killed off the red squirrels who had no immunity to this new disease. Second, the grey squirrels competed with the red, for their food source of green acorns. But when the acorns ran out, the grey squirrels could eat other foods too and continued to eat while the red squirrels could not. Lastly, the red squirrels reproduced much less as they were having to compete for food and thus, in some areas, the red squirrel died out altogether.

Populations of animals exist in delicate balance. For this reason, sometimes populations of animals are culled to avoid them becoming unstable and crashing. In Richmond Park, in London, where the animals are well protected from natural predators, the deer population is culled each year. Without this cull, the deer population would quickly increase. As the park size is limited, the food available is also limited. An oversized population of deer would quickly consume all the available food and then go hungry. Hungry animals have less body fat and often die in the cold winter months. An oversized population in close proximity is also more likely to suffer from a disease and the spread of disease in a close packed population would be quick and could be devastating. In addition, the plants eaten by the deer would be decimated by an oversized population of deer which would affect other animals that also rely on that food source. Therefore, culling is a responsible way to manage a herd in an enclosed environment.

Sadly, as our human population increases, we encroach more and more upon the natural habitat of other species, making their environment smaller, leading to the same problems as faced by the deer, left unmanaged, in a place such as Richmond Park.

The author of *The Last Wild*, Piers Torday, told me that one of the disease outbreaks that provided inspiration for the red-eye is a disease called myxomatosis that affects rabbits, and one of the symptoms is acute conjunctivitis which makes the eyes red and sore. This disease was actually used to cull rabbits. It was first used in Australia to control the ever increasing rabbit population in 1950 but it was also used in other countries. It spread to the UK in 1953 and was welcomed by farmers as rabbits were seen as pests as they ate the crops. But it was so effective that a large proportion of wild rabbits in the UK were killed and even now, domestic vets need a vaccine to protect them from contracting the disease from wild rabbits.

 ## ACTIVITY: Grass, rabbits and foxes

You will need:

- plastic tweezers (at least 30)
- dried beans (the smaller ones are the most challenging – small kidney beans work well)
- a tray with high sides (e.g. a classroom plastic drawer tray)
- small pots (or paper cups).

 ## Storify the science

Read from the part where Polly and Kester reach Old Barn Farm and realise The Wild is missing (p. 227). Keep going until you reach the part where Ma explains how the red-eye came and caused devastation and that she believes the source of the red-eye to be Kester's father.

Introduce the idea that the red-eye disease is based on a real disease and that myxomatosis still exists but doesn't affect any other species than rabbits. Reassure worried rabbit owners that there is a vaccine!

Draw a simple food chain of grass, rabbit, fox.

Discuss what would happen when it was a good year for growing grass, with just the right amount of rain and sunshine. There would be lots of grass and the rabbits would be well fed and the foxes would have plenty of food to eat.

Discuss what would happen if the foxes got red-eye?

Explain that we are going to find out what happens in different conditions.

 ## Set the challenge

(This is a game inspired by Clippy Island, by educators at Manchester University, on the BBSRC website which is fabulous if you are teaching evolution.)

You are going to model the rabbits feeding and see what happens in certain conditions.

- The beans are patches of grass worth one point.
- The tweezers are the rabbits.

Each child involved is a rabbit. They have a pair of tweezers and a pot. The rabbits have 30 seconds to pick up as many beans from the tray as they can and put them into a separate pot.

For every four points the rabbit gets, it can have a baby.

Keep a record of how many rabbits there are after every year that passes. You can plot it as a graph later. Use a table like this:

Season	Conditions	Population of rabbits	Number of rabbits eaten by foxes
Start		2	
End of Spring 1	Moderate grass growth		
End of Summer 1	Moderate grass growth		

We will have new players every round so that everyone can have a go.

Moderate grass growth

Spring 1 – an uneventful season of rain and sunshine with moderate grass growth. There are two rabbits and one fox.

In the tray – 20 beans

There are two rabbits.

Play the game with two children with one pair of tweezers each. Count up the points in the pot for each rabbit after 30 seconds. For every four points the rabbit scores, it can have a baby. Give out extra tweezers and pots to represent the babies.

The fox eats one rabbit for every ten rabbits so remove one pair of tweezers and a pot if necessary.

Note down how many rabbits there are at the end of Spring 1.

Summer 1 – another uneventful season of rain and sunshine with moderate grass growth.

In the tray – 20 beans in the tray

With new children (so that everyone has a turn), play the game with the number of rabbits left at the end of Spring 1. Count up the points after 30 seconds. For every four points the rabbit scores, it can have a baby. Give out extra tweezers and pots to represent the babies.

— If the population of rabbits is under ten then the fox will eat one.

— If the population of rabbits is over ten then the fox will eat two.

Remove tweezers and pots as necessary.

Repeat the same for **Spring 2** and **Summer 2**. The number of rabbits will go up and up until the food is no longer sufficient for the rabbits to have babies. Any rabbits with no beans will die so they must give their tweezers and pots back to the teacher. Note how many rabbits there are at the end of each season.

Keep going with **Spring 3** and **Summer 3** in the same way, always starting with 20 beans, until the population of rabbits is so great that they are all starving. As the tray isn't very big, there will be a certain amount of competition to even reach the food once there are six rabbits or so, so you may want to stop the game earlier.

Discuss how the population reaches a certain point and then it cannot grow anymore because the food becomes too scarce.

Drought – little grass growth

But what would happen if there was less food at the start?

We will replay the game in a time of drought. Put only ten beans into the tray but the rest of the rules remain the same. Start with two rabbits as before. Remember to write down how many rabbits remain at the end of each season.

Drought Spring 1 – there is little rain so the grass doesn't grow well.

In the tray – ten beans.

There are two rabbits.

Predict what might happen in **Drought Spring 1** and **Drought Summer 1**. Now play these two seasons to see if you were right.

Moderate grass growth and more foxes

What would happen if there were more foxes?

We will replay the game with more predators. Put 20 beans into the tray. Start with two rabbits as before but at the end of each season four rabbits are eaten. Remember to write down how many rabbits remain at the end of each season.

Extra predators Spring 1 – there is good rainfall and grass growth but foxes from a nearby farm have starting feeding on this farm too.

In the tray – 20 beans

There are two rabbits.

Four rabbits are eaten by foxes at the end of each season.

Predict what will happen and then play **Extra Predators Spring 1** and **Extra Predators Summer 1** to see if you were right.

Foxes catch red-eye

What would happen if the foxes caught red-eye?

Can you design the conditions that would represent this and predict what would happen? Now play the game for **Red-Eye Foxes Spring 1 and Summer 1** to see if you were right.

Game summary

Season	Conditions	Rabbit eaten by foxes at end of each season	Population of rabbits?
Start			2
Spring 1 Summer 1 Spring 2 Summer 2 Spring 3 Summer 3 Continue until population stabilises	Moderate grass growth – start each season with 20 beans	10 rabbits = 1 eaten by fox 20 rabbits =2 eaten by fox	Stabilises at high number
Drought spring 1 Drought summer 1 Keep going until population stabilises or all die out	Little grass growth – start each season with 10 beans	10 rabbits = 1 eaten by fox 20 rabbits =2 eaten by fox	Stabilises at low number
Extra Predators Spring 1 Extra Predators Summer 1 Keep going until population stabilises or all die out	Moderate grass growth – start each round with 20 beans	4 rabbits eaten at the end of each season	Stabilises at low number or all die out
Red-eye foxes Spring 1 Red-eye foxes Summer 1 Keep going until population stabilises or all die out	You decide	You decide	You predict

Finale

What would happen if the rabbits were reliant on a bee pollinated crop such as strawberries and the bees all caught red-eye?

Many of our food crops are pollinated by insect pollinators. Without pollinators, flowers wouldn't develop into fruit. Without this part of the reproductive cycle of plants, many plants would just stop growing. It sounds awful. And yet, there is something like this happening in our world. Bees are our main crop pollinators but they are under attack from the insecticides that farmers use on their crops, the loss of hedgerows at the edge of fields (where they can live) and from diseases.

What can we do? We can make our local habitat more bee friendly. Find out how to make a bee hotel or which plants you can safely put into your school environment to encourage bees to thrive. Even city areas can be bee friendly.

 Teacher's top tips

Hopefully, there will be enough rounds for everyone to have a go. Include children in the noting down of the numbers of rabbits and timing the 30 second intervals to keep everybody engaged.

If the game is too much for your class, play until you can see a pattern emerging in the numbers and then stop. There's no need to play every round.

When you get too many people around the tray for the game to work . . . stop!

If the tray is on a table rather than the floor, they are less likely to bang heads. Encourage sitting back and putting arms in to get the beans, rather than hovering heads over the tray.

You'll need enough tweezers for all the rabbits that you might end up with. There are cheap ones on the internet. You may find some in your bug hunting equipment or in the younger classrooms as they're excellent tools to teach fine motor skills.

What results should I expect?

If food is plentiful and there aren't too many predators then rabbit populations will increase and increase (as well-fed rabbits can reproduce more) until the food is insufficient to feed them all. Then some will die off and the population will level out at a stable number.

With less food, fewer rabbits can survive so the stable population will be smaller.

With a good food supply but more predators, the rabbit population will also stabilise at a lower level.

What next?

If you want to record your findings in a creative way then you could:

- Write a scientific report for Facto as if you were a scientist like Kester's father. Put your data into a bar chart and show how the population of rabbits grew and grew until there were so many that there wasn't enough grass for them all. For many rabbits to exist in a stable population there must be a lot of grass and not too many predators.

- Write a story where all the bees in a village get the red-eye and they die so that all the farmers' crops fail to produce seeds or fruit and the village goes hungry that winter. Devise a way that the farmer could solve this problem, so that he can grow crops again the next year and the villagers are saved.

- Role-play: being the General explaining to Kester how the red-eye caused the crops to fail by killing off the pollinators. Once you have practised it, write this conversation down as a script or film it. You could even record the voices afterwards on an app such as iMovie so that you can make it seem as if The General and Kester are speaking in their inner voices.

- Find out which crops are pollinated by bees. Work out what breakfast might look like without the foods pollinated by bees. Write a leaflet explaining why we should look after our bees, entitled 'Save our Breakfast!'

Assessing children's understanding

The following statements are indicators of basic understanding:

- When there are lots of rabbits, they run out of food.
- When there are lots of foxes, they keep the rabbit number down.
- When an animal population is affected by disease it can also affect any predator species.

More advanced understanding:

- The number of animals in a population is affected by lots of different things and is in a delicate balance.
- Populations stabilise at a number determined by food availability and mortality rate.

———————————————

FEAST

Story link
They are going to eat the stag.

 THE SCIENCE: Digestion

These are the facts that the children need to know, at a level appropriate for children of this age.

Digestion begins in the mouth when we bite off our food and chew it up into smaller pieces that we can swallow and break down in our stomachs. Our incisors slice off a piece (like scissors) and our tongue moves it to the back of our mouths to be crushed by our molars (like a potato masher).

When we swallow, the food moves down a long tube called the oesophagus. It will go down towards the stomach even if we stand on our heads as this tube is muscular and can push the food down the tube by contracting in waves called peristalsis. You can feel this if you put your hand on your neck and swallow.

At the end of the oesophagus is the stomach. The food passes into the stomach through a one-way valve so it doesn't all fall out if we do a hand stand. In the stomach, acid is secreted which makes the stomach environment perfect for the stomach enzymes to break the food down into smaller molecules. It is this acid that tastes so awful when we vomit.

(Not everything is broken down. Some fibrous things, such as sweetcorn, look the same on the way out as they did on the way in.)

Then, the food passes into the small intestine. Here, the molecules that are needed by the body, pass through the tiny holes in the intestine wall into nearby blood vessels so that the nutrition in our food can reach the rest of the body, in the blood.

When the food reaches the large intestine, water is absorbed from our food. Finally, the undigested food that is left over, after we have taken what we need from our food, is collected in the rectum until we feel the need to go! Then it is expelled through the anus.

 ACTIVITY: Modelling the gut

Thanks to Sarah Bearchell (*Sarah's Adventures in Science*) and Jon Wood (*Jon Wood Science*) for the following brilliantly disgusting activity.

You will need:

- Dolores – a model of the gut (I'll show you how to make her below!)
- an apron
- a large bowl
- a potato masher
- a pair of scissors
- a fork
- a pestle and mortar
- a large spoon
- a slice of bread
- a tin of spaghetti hoops
- a tin of sweetcorn
- a plastic box
- a packet of oats
- a litre bottle of cola
- instant coffee powder
- a large plastic milk bottle with integral handle
- a pair of thick tights 40 denier at least – without holes
- an inner tube from a bike tyre
- two pieces of rigid plastic tubing – I sawed the end off a watering can (minus the rose head)
- three jubilee clips
- good duct tape
- large trays to cover the tables!

You will need to mix up the oats and cola and a few spoonfuls of coffee powder the night before to let it form porridge.

How to make Dolores!

- Cut the bottom off the milk bottle, below the integral handle. This is the stomach.
- Make a cut across the inner tube so that the circular tube opens out into one long piece. Attach one end of the inner tube over the neck of the milk bottle with a jubilee clip or duct tape. This is the small intestine.

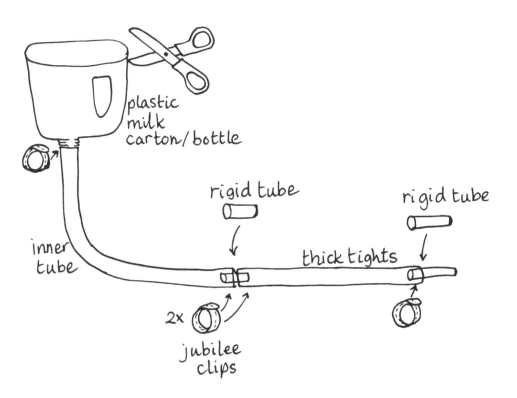

- Neatly cut one leg off the tights and cut off the sealed toe so you have another length of tubing made of tights! Thread a piece of rigid plastic tube into the free end of the inner tube. This will support the inner tube, keeping it open. Overlap the tights over the inner tube and rigid tube and fix it in place with the jubilee clip. The rigid tube in the centre should stop the jubilee clip from collapsing the tube and causing a blockage. You may need to stop the cut end of the tights fraying, using the duct tape. This is the lower intestine.

- Insert the last piece of rigid tubing into the open end of the tights and use a jubilee clip to hold it in place. This rigid tubing will form the rectum and the final opening – the anus.

 ## Storify the science

Read the story up to the point where the assembled people are calling for the feast and the stag is led forward (p. 243).

Discuss why the people are so frantic for real food. Discuss what it would be like to only eat Formul-A that tastes of prawn cocktail crisps and has no real texture.

Ask the children about their favourite food and how it feels to eat it. For example, I like the way cold, dark chocolate melts on my tongue.

Recall the part of the story where Kester eats real food for the first time (p. 105). It makes him sick as the berries are not edible for humans. What happens when you are sick? (This tends to get their attention!)

Discuss how, when we are sick, our body will eject whatever ails it as fast as possible. When we vomit, we also vomit foul-tasting acid because our stomachs need to be acidic to allow the stomach enzymes to break down our food.

Discuss how our bodies can also eject things from the gut in the other direction! When we have diarrhoea, our bodies hurry the process of our food passing through the gut and so we get little nutrition from our food and little water.

To understand how digestion works, we need to get a little messy!

How to run the activity

Make a long line of tables down the centre of the classroom and get the children sitting on either side, where they can see.

Lay Dolores out on the table, over trays. Make sure the tights section (large intestine) is over a suitably large tray (with sides as liquid will come out here).

At the head end, put the large bowl and masher. Put your apron on!

Do the following demo, following the script in **bold**:

- **First we take a bit of food. We chew it all up. Some bits of food get totally mashed up. Others stay in small chunks.**

Use scissors to demonstrate snipping off a bit of bread. Pour the pre-prepared oat, cola and coffee mix into the bowl, add the tin of spaghetti hoops and sweetcorn. Mash it up!

- **Then we swallow it. The food goes down the oesophagus and into our stomachs.**

    Ask a child to hold up the milk bottle (stomach) and use the other hand to squeeze the inner tube (small intestine) where it joins the milk bottle so that the food cannot pass out of the stomach until you are ready. Pour the mashed food into the milk bottle.

- **Acid and enzymes are squirted into the stomach to break the food down into molecules that can be absorbed later.**

- **Next, it passes into our small intestines. The intestines are a long tube that is coiled up inside our tummies. The walls of the intestines sit very close to tiny blood vessels so that the molecules of nutrients (like sugar) that our bodies need will pass through the intestinal walls and into the blood. This takes a long time. The food must be squeezed along this long tube.**

    The child can now let go of the top of the inner tube so that the food starts to drop into it. Ask a few children to take a turn at squeezing the food along the tube – don't squeeze it backwards into the stomach! Get all the food all the way down the tube, past the join and into the tights (large intestine). This bit will leak and be gooey and sticky.

- **After that, the food passes into our large intestine. It is here that all the water we need is absorbed. It comes out of the gut, through the walls of the large intestine and into our blood.**

    Start squeezing the food and let the sticky, oaty, cola juice come out through the tights. Keep squeezing until no more liquid comes out. Get any children who are willing to help you but be ready to wipe very sticky, drippy hands! If we don't poo regularly, then more water is extracted and our poo becomes dry and hard. This is constipation.

- **Finally, the waste from the food we eat that our bodies can't use has got to come out. It is stored in the rectum (the very last part of the tights/large intestine) until we are ready to release it! Then it comes out as poo when we go to the toilet.**

    Brace yourself for a disgusted audience as you squeeze out the poo through the rigid plastic tubing (anus). Notice that the sweetcorn still looks like sweetcorn as it is hard to digest and point out that this happens in real life!

 ## Teacher's top tips

Practise this at home so you can explain each part without having to refer to the script and try out the equipment so you know it won't spring a leak in the wrong place.

You can hose out the whole piece of equipment and hang it to dry to use again. Mine has lasted quite a few years.

It might get noisy. Make sure they can all see but not touch unless you ask them to – it can be pretty drippy!

Check that no child has an allergy before touching the food mix.

What next?

If you want to record your findings in a creative way then you could:

- Make a poster to go on the wall at Spectrum Hall. Draw the parts of the gut in sequence and label them. Annotate each part with an explanation of what part it plays in digestion.

- Make a model of the gut in dough and write labels for each part. Explain to a partner how it works.

- Role-play a conversation between Kester or Polly and the General. Explain to him how human digestion works.

- Film the process described above, or draw pictures, to represent each part. Write a script to use as a voice-over. Use an app such as iMovie to create a short film explaining human digestion. All mammals have a similar digestive system so you could make it quite simple so that the wolf cub can understand it. Or your target audience might be the children at Spectrum Hall.

- Kester and Polly eat cat biscuits (p. 141) as there is no other food left. Write the story of what happens to the cat biscuits as they travel through Kester's gut and why he feels more able to move after he has eaten.

 # Assessing children's understanding

The following statement is an indicator of basic understanding:

- I can name all the parts of the gut and put them in the right order.

More advanced understanding:

- I can explain what each part of the gut does to help our bodies absorb the nutrients and water from our food.

- I know that the food reaches the rest of our body via the blood.

A TRIAL DRUG

Story link

Kester and his father develop a trial drug to cure the red-eye.

THE SCIENCE: Teeth

Our teeth are adapted to efficiently chew up the food we eat. Carnivores eat other animals. Some carnivores will eat another animal whole but others must rip up their prey in order to eat it so they often have sharp, pointy teeth designed for shredding and tearing raw meat. Herbivores eat plants so they tend to have large blunt teeth for grinding their food. Omnivores, which eat both animal and plant matter, such as humans, have a mixture of these two types of teeth.

Front teeth – incisors
These cut and slice off chunks of the food.

Canines
In other mammals, these curved and pointed fang type teeth are good for spearing through prey and keeping hold of it if it struggles.

Back teeth – molars
These are large and wide for crushing. They may crush bones in carnivores or plant matter in herbivores.

The same is true for the beaks of birds. Meat eaters have sharper beaks to tear the flesh while seed eaters have strong, thicker beaks, capable of crushing.

RESEARCH AND DESIGN ACTIVITY: Design a route for Laura II

You will need:

- mirrors
- strawberries or another soft healthy snack (check for allergies)
- set of giant plastic/rubber teeth (available from online educational suppliers)
- skulls of animals (cleaned) if you can get them, or photos of animal skulls. You'll need: a deer, a cat, a wolf, a mouse and a pigeon. You can use any others you fancy
- reference books or natural history internet sites about animal skulls and teeth.

Storify the science

Read the first page of the last chapter. Continue to the point where Kester describes the trial drug that he has made with his father – Laura II. Later in the chapter, it describes the gel stick delivery method for this drug but don't read that far yet. Stop reading after the mention of the trial drug being tried on otters and polecats.

Ask the children how this medicine could be administered. They may suggest injecting the drug or feeding it to them in pill form. Encourage them to think about the practicalities of these methods – you would have to go out and find every animal. They may suggest putting it in food for the animals. Once the topic of food has arisen, point out that different animals eat very different things.

Show the children the fork, the scissors and the pestle and mortar. Play a game of 'Odd One Out'. Ask the children which is the odd one out and why. Any justified answer can be accepted. Hopefully they will note that the fork could be used for shredding, the scissors for snipping and the pestle and mortar for shredding. Leave the objects on the side where they can be seen.

Explain that we are going to investigate the way we eat so we can better understand how animals eat. Take a strawberry. Ask the children to instruct you how to eat it. Follow their instructions to the letter. The sequence you are looking for is:

- snip off a chunk of food with incisor;
- move food to the back of mouth with tongue;
- crush food with molars (to a pulp);
- swallow pulp.

Be playful and messy!

Now give them a strawberry and a mirror. Ask them to take a bite with their front teeth. Watch the upper and lower teeth work together like scissors. The word incisor is very like the word scissor. Now ask them to chew it up using their front teeth! Use the mirrors so they can see themselves. Is it easy? No!

Now, ask them to take a neat bite of the strawberry using their back teeth. Notice how the strawberry gets crushed.

Use the mirrors to observe their own teeth and show them (with a large picture or plastic model) all the different human teeth and learn to name them.

Look again at the fork, scissors and pestle and mortar. Ask the children which item is like which tooth type.

Now look at all the different animal skulls (or photos) to see how the teeth are different. Ask the children to name the teeth they can see.

Explain how animals that rip up their prey need sharp teeth for ripping and tearing the raw meat. Animals that eat grass, seeds and plant matter have to grind up their food to get the goodness out so their teeth are broad and flat and they may also have snipping teeth at the front to snip off the food.

Set the challenge

You are going to design a way for the trial drug to be delivered to animals by designing something they would be able to eat with the type of teeth they have. You could hide it in a type of food or find another way to get the animal to eat it.

Choose an animal that Kester would want to feed the drugs to:

- the stag
- the wolf
- the cat
- the mouse.

Find out about the teeth they have and what they eat.

Design a way to get the animal you want to save to eat the drug.

When you design your method, think about

- what the animal eats in the wild;
- what kind of teeth the animal has;
- how you will encourage the animal to **find** the drug;
- how you will encourage the animal to **eat** the drug;
- what shape and size and texture the drug should be so that it is eaten effectively.

Draw a diagram of the skull of your animal. Annotate it with labels, naming the types of teeth and their function.

Draw a diagram of the way you would encourage the animal to eat the drug.

 # Teacher's top tips

If you Google the question 'What does a stag eat?', you will get the answer shown below so this research is quite easy to do online. If you have no access to the internet then you may find the following information useful!

- the stag (herbivore – eats bark, twigs and leaves, nuts and fruit)
- the wolf (carnivore – eats large mammals such as deer or goats and smaller ones such as beavers)
- the cat (carnivore – eats small mammals and birds)
- the mouse (omnivore – eats grain, small insects, berries).

Let the children be creative. They may choose to trap the animals or lure them into a box where the food is released by a sensor etc.

They may want to include some talking animals, such as the pigeons, who can give instructions.

Accept all answers as long as the children have considered how to make sure the drug can be eaten by the animal of their choice. In order to consider this, they will have to observe the teeth and their form and function – which is the purpose of this task.

Finale

Return to the story and read on to the next page where the gel sticks are mentioned. Ask the children if they think this would work. Can they suggest any improvements? They might want to flavour the gel sticks to make them palatable to different animals.

At this point, you may want to find out about vaccines in real life. You could use the story of Edward Jenner who developed the vaccine for smallpox. It was a radical idea at the time but led to the eradication of smallpox. You can find the story told in many ways on the internet. There are some that are very child friendly. At the time of writing there is a nice one on the BBC Bitesize History website that has Edward Jenner narrating his own story.

What results should I expect?

The children should be familiar with names of all different types of teeth, their form and function.

 What next?

If you want to record your findings in a creative way then you could:

- Write a page to go in a book from Kester's father's laboratory – All About Teeth. Include diagrams and information about how the teeth are adapted to the food they eat.
- Role-play: Kester explaining to the pigeons about how to deliver the drug to the animal you chose, where to put it and what to say as instructions. Write the script for this scene. Make sure you include some nonsensical lines for the white pigeon! Or you could write this down as a set of instructions.
- Write an extra chapter to go at this point in the book. Describe the characters using your method for administering the drug but something goes wrong. Maybe the drug reaches the wrong animal and it doesn't have the right teeth to get to the drug. Describe how this problem is solved and decide whether the animal lives or dies.
- Write the story of Edward Jenner.

 Assessing children's understanding

The following statements are indicators of basic understanding:

- There are different kinds of teeth for eating different kinds of food.
- Incisors slice food.
- Molars crush food.
- Canines are for ripping and tearing.

More advanced understanding:

- The teeth we have reflect the food we eat because animals with teeth that are adapted to the food they eat are more likely to survive and have babies with teeth like theirs.
- Vaccines can be used to prevent sickness.

4 *Charlie and the Chocolate Factory*

(Roald Dahl, 1964)

It was the largest and most famous in the whole world! It was WONKA'S FACTORY, owned by a man called Mr Willy Wonka, the greatest inventor and maker of chocolates that there has ever been.

(Dahl, 1964, pp. 17–18)

TOPIC PLANNER

Story link	Science Changing materials	Activity	Page
Chocolate ice cream	Melting Experimental design Evaluating that design Thermal insulation Fair testing	Melting ice lollies (investigation 1) Wrapping ice lollies (investigation 2)	75 79
A palace made from chocolate	Melting chocolate Fair testing	Melting chocolate (investigation)	82–3
Mixing chocolate	Making bubbles – trapping gases	Making foam (investigation)	86
Gloop	Solid and liquids (and non-Newtonian fluids)	Running on gloop (observation and activity)	89
Fizz	Chemical reactions that produce gases Irreversible changes Chemical reactions that produce gases in a sealed unit Irreversible changes Changing one variable	Making sherbet (activity) Fizzy lifting drink rockets (investigation)	93 98

Story link	Science	Activity	Page
Gobstoppers	Factors that affect the speed at which sugar dissolves Reversible changes Designing a fair test	Dissolving sugar (investigation)	102
The furnace	Burning is an irreversible change Observing	Burning paper (demo) Trick candle (demo) Magic wish paper (demo)	106

CHOCOLATE ICE CREAM

Story link
Mr Wonka makes ice cream that doesn't melt.

THE SCIENCE 1: Melting

There are three states of matter: solid, liquid and gas. We can see these three states easily when we examine water: ice (a solid), water (a liquid) and invisible water vapour (a gas). See p. 112.

To change solid ice to a liquid, you need to add heat. To reverse this change in state you must cool it.

INVESTIGATION 1: Melting ice lollies

You will need:

- three different types of ice lolly per group – one large, ice-based lolly, one narrow ice-based one and one milk-based lolly. Ideally, they should all be the same length
- cups
- plastic tanks, trays or containers that won't leak

- tape, plasticine and other materials that could stick the lollies into place
- card or wood strips to make ice lolly stands
- accurate scales
- rulers.

Storify the science

Read Chapter 2 of *Charlie and the Chocolate Factory*, lingering over the mention of ice cream. Ask the children what their favourite flavour is. Discuss how difficult it is to eat ice cream on a hot day. Relate dripping ice cream to the melting of a solids to a liquid. Show the children an ice lolly. Can we see solid and liquid parts on these too?

Set the challenge

We may not be able to make ice cream that never melts but we can find a way to make ice cream treats last as long as possible.

You are going to investigate which qualities an ice lolly must have if it is not to melt too quickly in the sun.

You must set up the experiment to test which ice lolly lasts the longest. You'll need to collect some results to prove your answer.

When you design your test, think about:

- how to set up the lollies in order to observe them melting without touching them with your hands, which are warm;
- where to place the lollies to replicate a hot day;
- what you will measure;
- how you will measure it;
- ways to make the test fair.

Afterwards, think about what worked well and what you would do differently next time.

Teacher's top tips

Let the children set up their lollies and work out a way to measure the rate at which they melt. Most children will opt to measure the mass or volume of drips coming off the lollies or they will opt to measure the length of the remaining ice lolly with a ruler. This last method is most successful as mass and volume of small amounts of liquid are hard to measure with school equipment.

Don't worry if you can see that their experiment will fail. They will learn a lot from trying to make it work. Sometimes, they will set up something you can see is doomed, e.g. hanging ice lollies upside down from their sticks and you can see that the ice lolly will slip off. Let them try anyway! It is important to find out what won't work and to know why it won't work.

Spend time after the experiment discussing the method they used and evaluating their design.

Make sure you, the teacher, set up an experiment that will measure the length of the lolly every five minutes or so. This will yield a set of data that can be used by any group whose experiment didn't work!

Record your results in a table, e.g.:

Time (in minutes)	Length of lolly A	Length of lolly B	Length of lolly C
0			
5			

What results should I expect?

The larger the ice lolly, the longer it takes to melt. The larger the volume compared to the surface area, the longer it will stay cool. The heat can only reach the surface so one layer of the surface has to melt away to reveal the next layer underneath. The thicker the lolly, the more layers must melt away to get the heat to the cold centre and the longer the process takes.

Ice cream based ice lollies tend to soften faster and will become floppy and bend rather than dripping steadily like an ice-based lolly so it is harder to get a clear set of results with these lollies. They tend to look as though they will last for ages and then suddenly break.

What next?

If you want to record your findings in a creative way then you could:

- Role-play: being an Oompa Loompa in the Inventing Room tell Mr Wonka about your experiment and what you discovered. You could video this.
- Write a letter to explain to Mr Wonka which sort of lollies he should produce for the hot summer ahead and why.
- Write a letter to persuade Mr Wonka to make larger ice-based lollies.
- Write instructions on how to set up an experiment so that Mr Wonka can repeat your research.

Assessing children's understanding

The following statements are indicators of basic understanding:

- Solids may melt to a liquid when heated.
- Ice melts to liquid water when heated.
- The large ice lolly took the longest to melt.

More advanced understanding:

- The heat of the air in the room has supplied the energy to melt the ice lollies.
- The heat can only melt the outer layer of the ice lolly so it takes longer for the heat to reach the middle of the larger ice lollies so they melt more slowly.

Patterns they may be able to describe:

- The larger the ice lolly, the longer it takes to melt.

THE SCIENCE 2: Thermal insulation

We wrap up fish and chips to keep them warm on our journey home from the shop. The layers of material and the air trapped within prevent heat from transferring from the inside of the parcel to the outside. They insulate it. The more layers there are, the more air is trapped. Certain materials are good at trapping layers of warm air. They slow down how fast heat is lost from a warm body. We call them good thermal insulators.

This process can happen in reverse. When we use a cool bag to keep our food cool we trap layers of cool air around the food using thermal insulators which slows down the process of heat, from the outside, reaching the cold food.

If you left the ice cream or the fish and chips uncovered in a room, both would eventually reach the temperature of the room. The warmth of the air in the room would heat up the ice cream. The fish and chips would lose its energy to warm up the air in the room and thus cool to the same temperature as the room.

If we want to keep something hot or cold we must insulate it.

Children often think that layers placed around a cold substance will heat it up because our bodies feel warmer when wrapped in thick layers. But only warm things stay warm when wrapped. And human bodies continuously produce heat. The heat remains inside the wrapping. If a cold thing is wrapped, it will stay cold.

 ## INVESTIGATION 2: Wrapping ice lollies

You will need:

- pack of ice pops (frozen) – the type that are bags of liquids when not frozen – one per group
- A4 plastic wallet – one per group
- a selection of wrapping materials, e.g. paper, newspaper, net, thin fabric, fleece, bubblewrap, cotton wool, furry fabrics, tissue – enough for one type of material per group
- a set of accurate scales (which will measure to the nearest gram)
- a pair of scissors
- a bowl to catch the drips.

 ## Storify the science

Re-read Chapter 2 of *Charlie and the Chocolate Factory*, re-visiting the part about ice cream. Talk about buying an ice cream on a hot day. What if Mum wants one but she is at home. How could you get it home? We can't buy Mr Wonka's special ice cream so how can we stop ordinary ice cream from melting? Spend time talking about the cooler bags they use or how they could run quickly back. Listen to their ideas. Avoid giving them any firm answers – just listen with interest and ask what they know.

 ## Set the challenge

Mr Wonka wants to create special bags for ordinary ice creams like this (the sort that do melt in the sun). Which of these materials would allow the ice cream to melt most slowly?

Take a frozen ice pop and a plastic wallet for your group. Choose a material that you think will keep your ice pop coldest for longest. You can have as much material as you can get in the envelope, wrapped around your ice pop but no more.

At the end of the session (at least an hour) we will open the packages and see which ice pops are most icy!

Think about:

- which kind of material will keep the ice pop cool;
- how much of the material you want to use;
- how you wrap the ice pop up.

After an hour, your teacher will unwrap each in turn and cut a tiny hole in the bottom corner of the ice pop wrapper. They'll let the liquid drip out, leaving any ice and large slushy parts behind. Then they'll weigh the remaining ice pop on digital, reliable scales that will give you a reading to the nearest gram.

 ## Teacher's top tips

Children will often pick the netting. Let them! Making incorrect assumptions and getting unexpected results is half the fun in science. Some may even choose to have no wrapping at all. Again, let them!

Prepare a backup ice pop wrapped in as many layers of newspaper as you can fit into the plastic wallet without splitting it. You may want to do this after the children have done theirs – tell them you are joining in. This will yield a beautifully frozen ice pop, even after an hour.

If your class is motivated by a challenge, tell them they have to have more ice left than you do to win. Prepare your ice pop in newspaper in secret so they can't copy you.

What results should I expect?

The better the insulation, the more ice will be left. Newspaper works really well if there are lots of layers. Netting is wonderfully useless unless you use lots and lots of layers! Fleece, thick materials and bubblewrap trap plenty of air so they also work well, if they are well wrapped with plenty of layers. You could make a bar chart of the results. You could ask more able children to try using one layer of the material and compare it to two or three layers.

 ## Finale

This is a hard concept to learn as the children's experience tells them that you wrap up to stay warm not wrap up to stay cold!

Check their understanding by telling them that Mr Wonka ordered an ice sculpture for his grand opening. It arrived early. They didn't want it to melt . Two Oompa Loompas argued about what to do. One said they should put a blanket around it. The other disagreed. Who was right?

Discuss the problem and listen out for those children who have understood that the layers of blanket will insulate the sculpture and keep it cold.

What next?

If you want to record your findings in a creative way then you could:

- Write a laboratory report informing Mr Wonka of the results of the research with a recommendation for the type of material that makes the best thermal insulator for take-away bags.

- Role-play: being Mr Wonka and a worried customer who wants to take an ice cream home for a sick relative. Mr Wonka can reassure the customer that this take-away bag will work by explaining the science of thermal insulation.

- Design a bag and draw up an advert for your design, emphasising how the bags will keep the ice cream cold.

- Send your results to Mr Wonka. Write a letter to explain to Mr Wonka which sort of material he should use to make take-away bags and why.

St Cuthbert's School for Science Whizzkids
Physic Lane
Wonderbury

23rd June 2016

Dear Mr Wonka,

We have heard that you are interested in making special bags for taking your delicious ice cream home from your factory. We have been looking into this matter and thought you might like to hear the results of our research.

We found that newspaper is a great thermal insulator! We experimented by wrapping an ice pop in materials and leaving it for an hour to see if it melted. We tried all kinds of materials including net, fleece and furry fabric but newspaper was the best at keeping our ice pops icy which leads us to conclude that they will keep your ice cream cold too.

You will need to wrap the ice cream in a few layers of newspaper so that you trap air between the layers. These layers of paper and air trap the cold air inside and keep the heat out. As a result, the ice cream will remain frozen. Therefore, we suggest that you use newspaper to line the bags you make for your take-away ice creams.

Happily, newspaper is a very cheap resource as many people just throw it away. What a great way to recycle our old newspaper!

We hope you find this useful.

Yours experimentally,

Sara

Assessing children's understanding

The following statements are indicators of basic understanding:

- The ice pop must be wrapped to stay frozen.
- Thick materials kept the ice pop frozen.
- The ice pop in lots of layers of material stayed frozen longest.
- The unwrapped ice pops melted most quickly.

More advanced understanding:

- The heat of the air in the room takes longer to reach the ice pop when it is insulated with layers of fabric so the ice pop doesn't melt so fast.

Patterns they may be able to describe:

- Three layers of paper insulate better than two or indeed one so the more layers of a certain type of insulation, the longer the ice pop remains frozen.

A PALACE MADE FROM CHOCOLATE

Story link
Mr Wonka made a chocolate palace.

 THE SCIENCE: Melting chocolate

There are three states of matter: solid, liquid and gas. We can see these three states easily when we examine water: ice, water and invisible water vapour.

To change a solid to a liquid, you need to add heat to melt the solid.

Different materials melt at different temperatures. The three types of chocolate (white, dark and milk) melt at different temperatures too. The exact temperature depends on the ingredients in the chocolate so you may want to buy a few and try this test at home to find some that melt at obviously different speeds.

INVESTIGATION: Melting chocolate

You will need:

- three types of chocolate – approx. 5 g per group
- three small food bags per group
- trays or bowls of warm water (40 °C maximum for safety)
- timers – one per group
- thermometers – one per group
- jugs of spare warm water (40 °C) and cold water
- scales that will measure accurately to the nearest gram.

 # Storify the science

Read Chapter 3. Ask the children to imagine building a chocolate palace. What would the drawbacks be? Discuss the issues of sitting on chocolate chairs or trying to turn chocolate handles! Let them have time to talk to each other and come up with all the drawbacks they can think of – even the chocolate toilets!

Now, point out that Mr Wonka could choose which type of chocolate to build with. Which type would be best?

How do we define 'best'? Come to an agreement that, in this instance, the chocolate that melts most slowly is the best.

 # Set the challenge

You are going to test which chocolate melts most quickly. The warm water is for melting. Put the chocolate in bags so it doesn't mix with the water.

When you design your test think about:

- how you will know the chocolate has melted;
- what you will measure so you know which melted first;
- how you will make the test fair;
- how you will make sure you stay safe.

What did you notice?

Teacher's top tips

Let the children come up with ideas but you will need to guide them towards two basic experimental designs:

- Measure out equal quantities of chocolate into bags and time how long each one takes to melt by submerging in the water and squidging between their fingers. They could time one type of chocolate at a time.

- Measure out equal quantities of chocolate into bags and race all three at once and note which melts first, second and last.

Chocolate comes in various thicknesses and has differently sized squares. If you find three reasonably priced varieties, all by the same maker, with the same thickness and square size, you will make fair testing much simpler. If that is not possible – weigh the largest square and work out the equivalent weight in the other chocolates. Encourage the children to attempt to use the same amount in each test.

Buy a spare bar of milk chocolate to share at the end to discourage nibbling during the lesson!

What results should I expect?

One type of chocolate will melt more slowly than the others. Depending on the brand you use, it could be any type but the results for the class should be similar if they use the same three types of chocolate.

What matters is that they take a measurement of 'time taken to melt' for each chocolate or race all three at the same time and note which melts first, second and last as this will enable them to answer the question: which chocolate is best for building a palace?

If the children measure time taken to melt then they can create a bar graph of the results.

 ## Finale

To make your lesson really memorable, make three chocolate palace domes from the same three chocolates that the children are testing. Do this in advance of the lesson as this is not a suitable activity for a classroom full of children. These domes should only be prepared by an adult.

To make a dome, warm the chocolate and blow up a balloon. Put a little water into the balloon to stop it popping if the chocolate is very hot. Mark a straight line around the widest part of the balloon. Dip the balloon into warm molten chocolate up to the line and then allow to drip and place on greaseproof paper.

Repeat four or five times to cover half of the balloon in a thickish layer of chocolate and allow to cool. Pop the balloon to reveal a cup of chocolate. Trim carefully and place upside down to create a dome. Repeat with the other chocolate varieties.

Alternatively, do this experiment just before Easter and buy three Easter eggs in different varieties of chocolate. (If you want them to melt in the same order as the experiment then buy eggs made of the same chocolate as you used in the experiment.)

Now all you need is 'sunshine' to melt the dome on Prince Pondicherry's palace. For this you can use a hairdryer. Point the hairdryer, on the warm setting, at each dome in turn. Make sure the hairdryer is securely held in the same position for each test (operated by an adult) and that the children are not close enough to be splashed by melting chocolate. You may need to fix the domes to the desk to stop them blowing away! Time how long it takes to melt a hole in the side.

What next?

If you want to record your findings in a creative way then you could:

- Invite Mr Wonka (friendly adult in top hat) to class to hear a presentation on which chocolate would be best for building palaces and how we carried out our investigation.

- Write to Prince Pondicherry explaining why a chocolate palace is no more use than a chocolate teapot and persuading him to spend his money on something more useful.

- Design a marquee that could be erected over the palace to insulate it from the heat of the sun, using your knowledge of thermal insulators.

- Write a report for Mr Wonka on the differences between dark, milk and white chocolate and the way they could be best used in the building trade (i.e. which would make good cement, which would make the best bricks etc.).

Assessing children's understanding

The following statements are indicators of basic understanding:

- Solids may melt to a liquid when heated.
- The chocolate melts when it is heated.
- Some chocolate is harder to melt than others.

More advanced understanding:

- The heat of the hot air from the hairdryer has supplied the energy to melt the chocolate.
- The different chocolates melt at different rates because they have different ingredients which have different properties.
- A chocolate that melts more slowly will be more useful in building the palace because it will last longer in the heat of the sun.

Patterns they may be able to describe:

- The pattern will vary depending on the actual ingredients in the three types of chocolate. You will have to test them yourself. You may find that the darker the chocolate, the longer it takes to melt.

MIXING CHOCOLATE

Story link
The chocolate waterfall

THE SCIENCE: Making bubbles

There are three states of matter: solid, liquid and gas. Air is a mixture of gases. When we blow a bubble, it is easy to see that there is a gas present, as we can see that there is something going into the bubble as it forms and expands, even if we can't see the gas itself.

Foam is made from many tiny bubbles – pockets of gas trapped inside a liquid. When you make foam from washing up liquid and water, the surface of the bubbles is made from that mixture too.

INVESTIGATION: Making foam

You will need:

- tall measuring cylinders that can take at least 500 ml of fluid
- 500 ml beakers (plastic)
- spoons
- forks
- whisks
- water
- straws

- washing up liquid
- table covers or large trays or an outside space to work in
- pipettes that can measure 1 ml drops
- chocolate milkshake powder
- milk
- clean drinking cup

Storify the science

Read Chapter 15. Linger over the description of the chocolate waterfall. Imagine what it would smell like in that room.

Show them the chocolate milkshake powder and the milk. Ask them to imagine Mr Wonka making a chocolate milkshake. How do you think he would mix the powder to get the 'best' milkshake? What is the 'best' milkshake? Suggest that milkshakes should be foamy just like the chocolate river so our definition of the 'best' milkshake is the one with the most foam.

Demonstrate stirring the powder into the milk. Stir very gently so no foam is created. Ask 'Is it foamy?'

Ask the children to come up with ways to make it more foamy. They will suggest whisking. If they don't suggest it without prompting, remind them of the chocolate waterfall and that pouring from a height could make foam.

Discuss what is inside the foam. Draw attention to the fact that there is air trapped inside each bubble.

 ## Set the challenge

You are going to find out which mixing method creates the most foam. We're going to use water and washing up liquid to avoid getting milk everywhere.

When you design your test think about:

- which mixing methods you wish to test and the equipment you will need;
- how you will measure the foam;
- how much water and washing up liquid you use each time;
- how you will make your test fair.

 ## Teacher's top tips

This is a great session to do outside in the summer. When you have made lots of foam you may find it hard to wash it all away down the sink so you may want to collect it in a tub and let the foam pop before tipping away.

The tricky part with this test is to make it fair. The only thing you may be able to control is the length of time you mix for and the amount of water and washing up liquid you use each time: 300 ml of water to 1 ml of good quality washing up liquid can be enough to create plenty of foam.

Essentially, this is an activity where the children can try something out and observe what happens. They can also measure the foam but don't worry too much about accuracy. The most important thing is to encourage the children to notice that some methods introduce more air into the liquid, thus creating more foam. They could stir the mixture, whisk the mixture, blow bubbles with a straw or pour the mixture into a beaker from a height.

The best way to measure the foam is to pour the mixture and foam into a tall measuring cylinder and note where the top of the foam comes to in ml. It is easier to see in the measuring cylinder than the wider beaker but you may find some foams are hard to pour so test before you begin and decide what works best with the equipment you have to hand. You could even measure the height of the foam with a ruler.

Spend time discussing the fact that foam is made from a liquid and gas – two states of matter.

What results should I expect?

Any method that traps a lot of air in the liquid will create a good foam. Pouring the mixture from one beaker to another, repeatedly, mimicking the waterfall, creates a good head of foam.

 What next?

If you want to record your findings in a creative way then you could:

- Write a letter to persuade Mr Wonka to change his method of mixing chocolate. Do this if you found that whisking the chocolate created more foam than the waterfall method.

- Prepare a script for a children's science TV show, demonstrating the different ways to make the foam and explaining what bubbles are made of.

- Design a chocolate milkshake mixing machine. Draw your design and annotate it to explain the purpose of each part.

- Draw a bar chart of your results and write a report for Mr Wonka explaining which you think is the 'best' method for making a foamy chocolate milkshake. Refer to your results to support your ideas.

 Assessing children's understanding

The following statement is an indicator of basic understanding:

- There is air inside the bubbles.

More advanced understanding:

- The air inside the bubbles is preventing the bubble from collapsing.
- The air inside the bubbles is a gas.
- Gases take up space.
- The foam is formed when air is trapped inside the liquid.

Patterns they may be able to describe:

- The mixing methods that introduce more air into the liquid make more foam.

GLOOP

Story link
Augustus Gloop is sucked up the pipe.

THE SCIENCE: Solids and liquids

Liquids have certain properties. Their particles are loosely bonded together and will flow. They have a fixed volume and tend to take up the shape of the container they are in. If you drop a stone into a liquid such as water, which is not as dense as stone, the stone will make a splash and quickly sink to the bottom.

Solids have certain properties. They are firmly bonded together and will keep their shape regardless of the container. If you drop a stone onto a solid, such as ice, it will bounce and then remain on the top of the solid.

Gloop, like custard and ketchup, is a non-Newtonian fluid. These fluids behave differently from most liquids and sometimes behave like solids. Newton described how fluids should behave in different situations and these non-Newtonian fluids simply don't obey the rules! If you apply a force they may appear to become thicker (more viscous) like gloop, or runnier (less viscous) like ketchup. This is why you have to tap the bottle to get ketchup out.

ACTIVITY: Running on gloop

You will need:

- cornflour (corn starch) – enough to half fill the tank you wish to run on
- two plastic tanks – large enough to fit
  a pair of feet with space around them – 10–20 litre capacity should be big enough
- water
- smaller trays if you want the children to handle the gloop
- wooden spoon
- 200 g mass
- sealed jar of water
- sealed jar of sugar
- sealed jar of plastic cubes.

Read Chapters 15, 16 and 17. Create a sense of amazement that a whole environment can be edible. Ask the children what they would eat first. Ask them what they think will happen to Augustus. Gloop is a great word – ask them to describe what they think gloop looks like. Tell them we are going to find out more about gloop.

How to organise the lesson as a demonstration

Get your large tank of gloop ready.

Show the children with a jar of water, a jar of sugar and a jar of plastic cubes or bricks. You could play 'Odd One Out' as described on p. 114 in the Kensuke chapter. Look at the way the water pours and changes shape but the cubes stay cube shaped. Take the cubes out and make a tower. Discuss whether this is possible with water or sugar. Elicit from them a definition of a solid and a liquid.

Now look at the gloop. Tip the tank side to side and let them watch the gloop slowly flow in each direction.

Ask – Is it a solid or a liquid?

Ask for a volunteer to sit next to the tank. Get a strong wooden spoon and bang it down on the surface of the gloop. If you have made it to the right consistency, it will not splash but the child will flinch thinking they're about to get covered in gloop.

Ask – Is it a solid or a liquid?

Put your hand into the gloop and pick up a handful. Let it drain through your fingers. Then grab some more and roll it in your hands, applying pressure and then snap the roll of gloop in half.

Ask – Is it a solid or a liquid?

Drop the 200 g mass onto the gloop from a height of about 1 metre. You should be able to get it to bounce before it sinks slowly into the gloop.

Ask – Is it a solid or a liquid? (Notice that it behaves like a solid when under pressure.)

Ask – What do you think would happen if we stood on it?

Now, one by one, let them step quickly onto the gloop, barefoot and start running. Don't stop running. Then get straight out and into the foot bath without stopping.

Ask – How did that feel? Did it feel solid or liquid?

Take lots of photos!

Explain that some substances behave in this way. They appear to be liquids because they flow but if you apply a force to it, they act like a solid. They are called non-Newtonian fluids. Discuss this and how it differs from the way most liquids and solids behave.

Teacher's top tips

Gloop will wash out and it will dry out and brush out of carpets etc. That said, it is REALLY MESSY!

You can make gloop by slowly adding water to cornflour, much as you would when making custard from powder. Keep adding the water until it just becomes liquid. To begin with it will make a very firm and squeaky, lumpy, powdery dough, but as you add more water, it relaxes into a thick liquid. You want to achieve the thickest liquid to can make, with no splashy liquid on the top. Mixing it is hard work and takes time so leave plenty of preparation time for a large batch.

When you get rid of gloop, leave it to settle so that the water comes to the top and you can pour it off. Then scrape the flour into a bin – it will clog drains!

When you prepare this lesson, also prepare a footbath and have a towel ready and have a waterproof mat covering the floor (or go outside).

If you don't mind the mess on clothing, you could get each group of children to prepare their own gloop following your instructions (practise first). They really enjoy the process, and then you can put all their batches together to make one big one to run on.

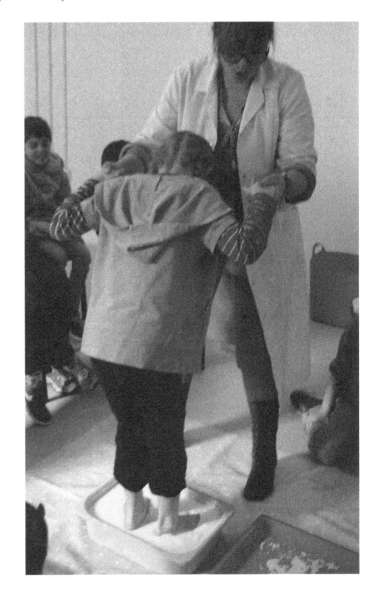

When you get to running on gloop, this must be done quickly. Step on and start running. Do this one child at a time and hold their hands. Do not let them stop running as they will sink to the bottom and it is quite hard to get out. Then, get them to step directly into a foot bath of warm clean water where they can wash off the gloop and then dry their feet.

Avoid filling the tank more than 10 cm high so that you can't sink too far into it. It is hard to get out!

If you do accidently sink into the gloop, use your hands to let air into the space around the foot to help release it. Always get feet out straight-away as the gloop is heavy on little feet.

What next?

If you want to record your findings in a creative way then you could:

- Write a fact sheet about solids sand liquids and how they behave. Include a section on gloop!

- Role-play: being a gloop expert prepare a presentation on solids and liquids and include a demonstration of how you can run on liquids if they are non-Newtonian.

- Role-play: being a new reporter at the scene of the 'Augustus Gloop going up the pipe' incident. Include a scientist's report into what has become of Augustus and whether gloop can be classified as a solid or liquid.

- Dip strawberry fudge in melted chocolate to sell at the next fundraiser. Note which ingredients remain as a solid and which melt.

Assessing children's understanding

The following statements are indicators of basic understanding:

- Solids have particular properties, e.g. they keep their shape.
- Liquids have particular properties, e.g. they can be poured.
- Gloop sometimes behaves like a solid and sometimes like a liquid.

More advanced understanding:

- When a force is applied to the gloop, it behaves like a solid.
- When we run on the gloop, we are exerting force on it with our feet and it behaves like a solid so we stay on top.

Patterns they may be able to describe:

- The harder you hit the gloop, the more viscous (thick) it becomes.

———————————————

FIZZ

Story link
Mr Wonka makes drinks that lift you up.

THE SCIENCE 1: Chemical reactions that produce gases

When some substances are mixed, they will react together to form a new substance. When you mix vinegar (an acid) with bicarbonate of soda (baking soda), carbon dioxide gas is released. It forms as bubbles in the liquid that surface and pop, releasing carbon dioxide into the air.

This change is irreversible as the gas is lost. You cannot put the gas back.

When you mix citric acid (dried) with bicarbonate of soda and water, a similar reaction occurs and carbon dioxide is produced. The first two ingredients are present in sherbet so when we put it in our wet mouths, these bubbles form fizzing foam on our tongues.

ACTIVITY 1: Making sherbet

You will need:

- icing sugar
- bowls (enough for one per pair of children)
- a spoon for each bowl
- clean hands
- bicarbonate of soda
- citric acid (available from the pharmacist)
- pestle and mortar
- vinegar
- sandwich bags
- washing up liquid
- matches (for adults only)
- small candle
- tall, narrow glass or glass jug/bottle (for adults only)
- tray to catch the drips
- digital microscope (optional).

Storify the science

Read Chapter 22, stopping as you reach the mention of fizzy lifting drinks. Ask the children how they think the drinks worked. As the word 'gas' arises in the conversation, ask them how the gas got inside the people and how the drinks were made fizzy. Listen to all their ideas without offering an explanation. Tell them you are going to investigate this fizz a little more.

How to organise the lesson as a demonstration

Demo – making fizz

Foamy recipe

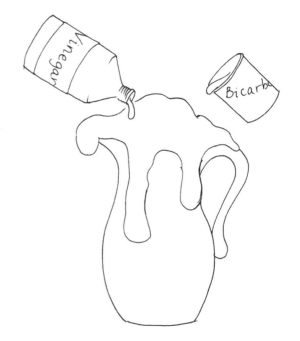

- a small squeeze of washing up liquid
- a few drops of food colouring
- two teaspoons of bicarbonate of soda
- 100 ml of vinegar

Take the tall glass jug and put a little of the washing up liquid in the bottom (this makes the foam last longer) and the food colouring. Now add the bicarbonate of soda. Lastly, pour in a few centimetres of vinegar. The mixture will foam up and hopefully start pouring, dramatically, down the sides of the jug.

If your class like comedy, pretend you were not expecting this and panic a little while you search for your tray to put under the jug to catch the drips.

Ask – what do you think is happening?

Talk about what is inside the bubbles. Once they have exhausted their ideas you can tell them that, unlike the foam they made before by whisking, the bubbles are not air – they are full of carbon dioxide.

Make another batch without the washing up liquid as the foam won't last and it releases the carbon dioxide into the jar.

Recipe with less foam

- two teaspoons of bicarbonate of soda
- 100 ml vinegar

When the foam subsides, take a lit match and lower it into the jar. If there is still carbon dioxide trapped inside, it will put the flame out. Carbon dioxide is heavier than air and will stay in the jar if it is not agitated too much.

If you pour carefully, you can actually pour the carbon dioxide gas out over a lit candle and put the flame out. Practise this before you do it in front of a class. (It's easy to pour vinegar and bicarb mix all over the table by mistake, putting the flame out!) You may need to empty the jug and start again for this bit so that there is less liquid in the jug.

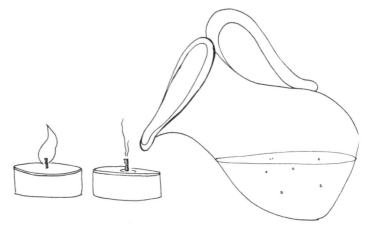

Teacher's top tips

Practise first so you know how much washing up liquid, bicarbonate of soda and vinegar to add to get the foam to spill over the top and how to pour the carbon dioxide over the tealights without spilling the liquid.

Put the tealights on the edge of the table so you can get the spout of the jug close to the flame without upending the jug and spilling vinegar on them.

Activity – making sherbet

Now give out the mixing bowls and spoons and ensure the children have clean hands. Tell them we are going to make a fizzy food. We can see if it lifts us! Discuss what it might be and tell them we are going to make sherbet.

Ask – What ingredients might we need?

They will usually start with sugar. Give out two heaped tablespoons of icing sugar per bowl. Let them taste a little without spreading germs by sprinkling some sugar from the bowl into their hand and licking it up from there.

Ask – Did it taste like sherbet? Did it fizz?

It doesn't fizz and it has no sour taste.

Ask – What could we add to make it taste more like sherbet?

They may offer the answer of lemon juice – citric acid is present in lemon juice. Citric acid has been dried so it won't react with anything until it is in water. Let the children taste one tiny granule each. (It's very sour.)

Ask – What does it taste like? Did it fizz?

Grind the citric acid granules to a powder so it will mix well. Put a level teaspoon of the powder into each bowl. Mix well and sprinkle a little onto their hands to taste (checking first for allergies).

Ask – What does it taste like now? Did it fizz?

It tastes more like sherbet but doesn't fizz.

Ask – What makes things fizzy?

Discuss the fact that there need to be bubbles. Recall the vinegar and bicarbonate of soda. If they suggest vinegar you can tell them that vinegar is a 'wet' acid while citric acid is a dry one. You need a dry one in sherbet. Once they have worked out that they need bicarbonate – let them taste a little. Be sparing. It's not nice!

Ask – What does it taste like? Did it fizz?

Add a level teaspoon of bicarbonate into each bowl and mix. Taste a little.

Ask – What does it taste like now? Did it fizz?

Now the children should experience the fizz on their tongues. You can bag up the sherbet and send it home with them. If you're feeling generous, provide a lollipop to dip with!

If you have a hand held digital microscope, you can put a little sherbet on a tray, add water and watch the bubbles form with the microscope.

Relate all this back to the reaction with vinegar and bicarbonate of soda and emphasise that carbon dioxide is formed which makes the bubbles and this is an irreversible change because the gas is lost to the air.

 ## Teacher's top tips

Let the children make their own portion of sherbet if you can tolerate the excitement and the inevitable dusting of icing sugar on everything. If mess is a problem, then do this as a demonstration in one bowl at the front, with enough sherbet for everyone to taste all the ingredients and have a little sherbet to take home.

Be aware that some children may be allergic to the ingredients. Occasionally children are intolerant of citrus fruits and therefore citric acid so do check this before you begin.

You may be lucky enough to have a school kitchen where you can make the sherbet. If so, remember that the discussion and working out the ingredients is the most important part.

 ## What next?

If you want to record your findings in a creative way then you could:

- Role-play: being Mr Wonka. Explain to Grandpa Joe and Charlie how to make sherbet. Use this to help you write instructions or a recipe.
- Draw a cartoon strip of the process of making sherbet, explaining each step and the science of what is happening.
- Find other fizzy foods and drinks and research their ingredients to find out how they fizz. Make a fizzy food fact file.

 ## Assessing children's understanding

The following statements are indicators of basic understanding:

- Sherbet fizzes because there are bubbles of gas being produced.
- The gas is carbon dioxide.

More advanced understanding:

- The sherbet fizzes because there is a chemical reaction happening.
- Carbon dioxide is produced when an acid is mixed with bicarbonate of soda.
- This process is irreversible because the gas is lost to the air.

THE SCIENCE 2: Chemical reactions that produce gases in a sealed unit

Bubbles are produced when the dry ingredients in an effervescent tablet come in contact with water. These tablets often contain citric acid and bicarbonate of soda so, as with sherbet, carbon dioxide is produced.

Once the lid of the pop rocket pot is firmly clicked into place, the gas bubbles are released into this sealed unit. As more gas is released, the pressure builds up and the pot will eventually break open at the weakest point – the seal on the pot, shooting the upmost part upwards. The better the seal, the longer the pot will stay together and the more impressive the pop!

INVESTIGATION 2: Fizzy lifting drink rockets

You will need:

- film canisters – one per pair (You can get these on the internet. The ones that seal best and fly the highest have a lid that fits inside the base not over the top – see diagram.)
- effervescent tablet (Choose one with no medicines or cleaning chemicals. I use vitamin C tablets.)
- water in beakers
- safety goggles, if you feel they are necessary
- a large, open air space.

Storify the science

Remind the children of Chapter 22 and their previous discussion about how fizzy lifting drinks might work. Mr Wonka had not yet perfected the fizzy lifting drink.

Imagine what it would feel like to lift off. The original film shows a scene where Charlie and Joe drink the lifting drink and take off. You could show that here. Take the children outside and seat them at least a couple of metres from where you are going to fire your first fizzy lifting drink rocket. Set off your first rocket (see below for instructions) and ask the children what they think happened.

Set the challenge

You are going to see if you can make a fizzy drink lift Charlie to a particular height.

You have to make your drink lift Charlie higher than mine.

When you set up your fizzy lifting drink rocket think about:

- how much water you put in the pot;
- how much tablet you put in the pot;
- which pot you choose;
- how you can make it go higher;
- staying safe.

What made the rocket go highest?

 # Teacher's top tips

To set off a rocket you must start with your chosen amount of water in the rocket. Prepare one in advance with about one third of the canister filled with water but don't let the children see how much you have added. This will get a high launch. Add half a tablet and click the lid firmly on. Place it lid downwards on a flat piece of ground and stand back and wait. It won't take long to pop and send the pot flying upwards. If you have Charlie drawn on the side of the pot, you'll send him flying skywards.

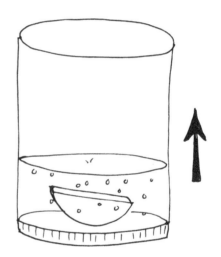

These little pots can go off with quite a force so you will need to consider safety. If your class are very excitable, you may need to do this in smaller groups or with more adults.

Before you give out equipment, establish the routine:

- enter the testing zone (mark off one side of the playground);
- practise clicking the lid on properly! it can be tricky and cause panic;
- add water to the empty pot;
- countdown so everyone adds tablet at the same time;
- click the lid on and place upside down on flat surface;
- retire immediately to the safety zone (mark off the opposite side of playground) to watch the display;
- if yours is not ready, leave it and go to the safety zone.

Children are easily excited, so make sure there is a good distance (5 metres or more) between the testing zone and the safety zone.

It is hard to measure the heights – especially in the wind! So, just encourage the children to note whether theirs has gone higher or lower than the last test.

Strong winds may knock the pots over so avoid windy days.

Although the best pots are the ones shown above, you may want to include pots with lids that do not seal so well as this could be another variable to investigate.

Encourage the children to change one variable at a time so they can identify the effect.

After each launch take time to reflect on what they learned from that launch and what they want to try next.

What results should I expect?

There are lots of variables in this experiment that can make a difference to how high or how quickly the rocket goes off. Variables that affect height:

- the strength of the pot seal – pots go higher if the lid seals better as the seal holds until the pressure is higher, propelling the pot a longer way;

- the amount of water – if there are only a few drips of water, no bubbles are produced and nothing happens. If there is too much water then there is no airspace for the gas to build up. The optimum height is achieved with the pot about a quarter filled with water so there is plenty of airspace in which the gas can build up;

- the size of the pot – larger pots (like the tubes you buy effervescent tablets in) are heavy to lift and tend not to go very high.

Variables with other effects:

- the amount of tablet – as long as there is enough tablet to create sufficient gas, the rocket will go off eventually. Any extra is wasted so you may want to use half tablets;

- the size of the tablet particles – crushed tablets have more surface area of tablet available to react so the whole reaction happens faster;

- shaking the pot – shaking the pot after the tablet is added can make the reaction happen faster as the ingredients are mixed more thoroughly;

- the temperature of the water – the reaction happens more quickly when the water is warmer.

In this investigation, we want to find out which variables lift the pot the highest like the lifting drink but you may want to extend this investigation and find out which make the rocket go off most quickly – the time taken to pop is much easier to measure than the height.

What next?

If you want to record your findings in a creative way then you could:

- Role-play: being two naughty Oompa Loompas messing about with Fizzy Lifting Drink. Tell each other how you're going to make your pot go really high.

- Film the pots in slow motion and use the images in a training seminar for Mr Wonka and the Oompa Loompas on the results of your research.

- Write a report on the way to make the fizzy lifting drink rockets reach their full potential height. Explain why the amount of water, tablet and seal on the pot affect the height of the rocket.

- Role-play: being reporters reporting on the 'Highest known flight of the Fizzy Lifting Drink Rocket'. Include an interview with the scientists who explain how they made it go so high.

Assessing children's understanding

The following statements are indicators of basic understanding:

- Gas is trapped inside the canister and it pushes the lid/base off.

- The rockets go higher when the pots are about a third full of water.

More advanced understanding:

- The tablet dissolves and reacts with the water and bubbles of carbon dioxide gas are produced.

- The gas can only build up in the air-filled cavity, not where the water is present so filling the pot with water stops it going high.

- The particles of gas are pushing in all directions but the only place the pot can break is at the seal.

- The seal breaks due to the pressure of the increasing amount of gas inside.

- The pressure of the gas inside propels the lid down and the base of the pot upwards.

Patterns they may be able to describe:

- The greater the airspace, the more gas can build up so the greater the pressure and higher the rocket goes (as long as there is sufficient water to dissolve the tablet and the pot is not big or heavy).

- The better the seal on the pot, the higher the pressure it can withstand before it pops and the higher it goes.

———————————————

GOBSTOPPERS

Story link
Mr Wonka makes Everlasting Gobstoppers.

THE SCIENCE: The factors that affect the speed at which sugar dissolves

When sugar is mixed with water it dissolves. The bonds between the sugar particles are broken so the sugar breaks down into much smaller pieces that cannot be seen or filtered out of the solution. The sugar is still present but we cannot see it.

Dissolving happens faster if the water is hot because the water molecules have more energy to move around and find new sugar particles to interact with. The same is true if energy is introduced by stirring the mixture.

Large crystals of sugar take longer to dissolve because the water can only reach the outside of the sugar crystal so crushing it up into smaller pieces increases the surface area of the sugar so more surface area is in contact with the water, increasing the speed at which it dissolves.

INVESTIGATION: Dissolving sugar

You will need:

- gobstoppers, the larger the better!
- small colourful sweet with a sugar shell, e.g. skittles
- clear glass jars
- water
- spoons
- beakers
- different types of sugar (e.g. large crystals, granulated and icing sugar)
- timers
- accurate measuring scoops (I use the ones you get with baby milk powder)

Storify the science

Read Chapter 19. Place a gobstopper and the smaller coloured sweet into clear glass jars of water so you can clearly see what happens. Leave them where you can see them for the day. Discuss what happens when you eat a gobstopper. Ask where does it go? Why does it get smaller? How could you make it last as long as possible? What is it made of? Make sure you discuss dissolving and make the point that the gobstopper in the jar is not disappearing – the sugar is dissolving. We can't see it but it is still there. If the water and jar are clean, you could taste the sugary water. Ask what can we do to the gobstopper in the jar to make it dissolve faster? Elicit some possible variables. Make sure you discuss heat, stirring and the size of the sweet – the smaller sweet may well have dissolved by now!

 # Set the challenge

You are going to find out what makes gobstoppers last as long as possible. They are mostly made from sugar so we will be working with sugar. There are lots of variables that might make a difference. You can't change them all as we need to know which one is making the difference.

When you design your test think about:

- which variable to investigate (hot/cold water, stirring/not stirring, large/small sugar grains);
- how to make sure you get some results within the time!
- what to change and what to keep the same to make your test fair;
- what you will measure;
- how you will know all the sugar is dissolved;
- how you will present your results to make them really clear so that others will understand what you did and what you found out.

 # Teacher's top tips

The basic idea here is to time how long it takes for the sugar to dissolve. One teaspoon of sugar in 200 ml of water is a sensible testing size but let them make some of these choices for themselves.

There may be some trial and error here in their experiment design. For instance, if they try putting a huge spoonful of sugar in cold water and not stirring, it could take hours to dissolve. You may want to let the children try their design and then allow time to discuss and redesign! They will only have a sense of how fast the sugar dissolves when they've tried it themselves.

You can stir the hot/cold water and big/small sugar crystal tests as long as you always stir the same amount (e.g. 20 times round the cup in 20 seconds).

Hot water from the tap is plenty hot enough to speed up the process of dissolving but always check the temperature is not going to scald.

Sugar cubes are made of granulated sugar stuck together. You get a much longer time taken to dissolve if you use the large crystal sugar used for coffee or decorating cakes.

Don't worry if the children get no data – you can always use the data from a group that got some clear results.

You can do as many tests as you like, e.g. water at 50, 40, 30, 20 and ten degrees but for some children, one hot and one cold will be enough! You could try three differently sized grains of sugar. Remember to keep all the other variables the same for a fair test.

Encourage the children to discuss what went well in their test and what they would do differently if they did it again. And you may want to repeat the whole experiment just to allow them the satisfaction of getting it right now that they know what to do.

Icing sugar tends to clump, so the manufacturers add anti-caking agents but these are not soluble so they make the solution cloudy. In this experiment, ignore the cloudiness and when there is no more solid icing sugar in the pot, stop the timer!

What results should I expect?

Sugar dissolves faster if you stir it or if the water is warmer and if the grains are smaller. So, to make a gobstopper last as long as possible, it should be enormous, and be placed in a very dry mouth and not stirred or moved around by the tongue. This can lead to some great discussions about how this might be made possible and hazard free!

What next?

If you want to record your findings in a creative way then you could:

- Send a full lab report to Mr Wonka explaining the significance of your results to the development of everlasting gobstoppers. Include graphs and a statement about the way to achieve gobstopper longevity.

- Design gobstoppers for Mr Wonka, explaining all the choices you made about size, flavourings (they mustn't make your mouth water) and instructions for eating.

- Write a letter to Mr Wonka persuading him to produce 'almost everlasting gobstoppers'. Explain how these might be made and point out that selling everlasting sweets will eventually put him out of business.

 Assessing children's understanding

The following statements are indicators of basic understanding:

- Sugar dissolves in water.
- When it dissolves you can't see it anymore but it is still there.
- Heating the water, stirring and crushing the sugar will make it dissolve faster.
- Gobstoppers are made of sugar and dissolve in the water in my mouth.

More advanced understanding:

- When sugar dissolves it breaks down into tiny particles that are too small to see.
- Heating the water and stirring make the molecules of water move faster so they reach the sugar more quickly and so the sugar dissolves more quickly.
- Water can only reach the outside of the big sugar crystals/gobstoppers so it takes time to dissolve away the outer layers and then dissolve the middle.

Patterns they may be able to describe:

- The hotter the water, the faster the sugar/gobstopper dissolves.
- The more you stir, the faster it dissolves.
- The smaller the gobstopper/sugar grains, the faster it dissolves.

THE FURNACE

Story link

Veruca misbehaves in the nut room.

THE SCIENCE: Burning is an irreversible change

When a material burns, there is a chemical change. Two molecules come together and form something new. When you burn paper, the oxygen in the air combines with the carbon and hydrogen in the paper. Carbon dioxide (CO_2) and water (H_2O) are formed and they escape as gases. Ash is left, which may be in tiny particles and be carried away in the smoke.

The ash and gases cannot be changed back into paper so the process is irreversible.

There are two parts to a candle – the wax and the wick. When a candle is burned, the wick will initially turn black as it is burning to begin with. Then, as it warms the wax, liquid wax begins to tap up the wick. It is heated by the flame and becomes a vapour. Now, it is this vapour that is the fuel for the flame so the candle eventually burns away. You can solidify the wax from liquid wax but the wax that has been burned as a vapour cannot be changed back to solid wax again – it has changed, irreversibly. Just like the paper and the wick, candle wax is made mostly from hydrogen and carbon. The hydrocarbons in the wax react with the oxygen and produce carbon dioxide and water which escape into the air and are lost.

A trick candle wick contains tiny particles of magnesium – a highly reactive metal. When you blow out the candle, the wax vapour is still present for a moment or two and only needs a tiny spark to relight it. The magnesium particles, hidden in the wick will continue to spark as they are hot enough to ignite and now exposed to oxygen. This spark relights the wax vapour almost instantly.

DEMO: Burning paper

You will need (all for adults only):

- a tealight
- a trick candle
  (relighting candle)
- large glass jar/drinking glass
- small drinking glass
- really large or really tiny drinking glass

- plate
- tongs
- posh tea-bag/floating wish paper
  (available on the internet)
- paper
- matches

Storify the science

Before you start, check the rules on lighting candles in your establishment and the location of any fire alarms. Nothing ruins a demo like a fire alarm. You may want to make sure the windows are open too!

Read Chapter 24. Veruca Salt and her parents end up down the rubbish chute on their way to the furnace. A harsh punishment but the furnace may not be lit . . . Ask the children to describe how they imagine the furnace and how it works. Elicit that it is likely to be coal or gas fired and will reach a high temperature, thus burning up and getting rid of all the rubbish.

Ask the children what happens to the rubbish and what might be left over. They are likely to tell you there is ash left.

Burning paper demo

Light a tealight candle, where they can all see the flame clearly. Using tongs, hold a small piece of paper up to discuss. Ask the children what they will see if you put it in the flame. Put the paper in the flame and observe. Discuss the fact that the paper burns away leaving only ash and smoke.

Now scrunch up another piece of paper (the same size as before) and set it on the plate. Set it alight and place the larger glass over it. Ask the children what they notice. They should see:

- smoke trapped in the glass;
- some condensation on the glass;
- the flame goes out before the paper is all burned;
- ash.

Discuss why the paper goes out. They may be aware that oxygen is required for things to burn. Explain that the carbon and hydrogen in the paper have combined with the oxygen to produce carbon dioxide and water vapour, both of which have escaped into the air and cannot be made back into paper.

Now repeat the process, only this time have a smaller glass ready. You may want to predict with the children what will happen. The paper will go out more quickly. Ask the children why they think this happened. Elicit that there is less oxygen in the smaller glass. Lead them to the relationship – the more oxygen, the longer the flame will burn. Now produce a larger glass and repeat. Hopefully the children will predict that the larger glass has more oxygen so the flame lasts longer. If you'd like data to record – repeat the demo with each glass and time how long it takes the flame to go out. Alternatively, put a lit tealight under each glass and see how long it takes to go out.

If you want to extend this into a maths activity, measure the capacity of each glass by measuring the amount of water required to fill it to the brim. Then time how long it takes for the flame to go out after the glass is put over it. Plot this data as a line graph (capacity of jar x time to go out). You should be able to use this line to predict intermediate values as you can produce another jar at the end and use the line to predict (from the capacity) how long the flame can remain alight.

Discuss that the furnace can't be sealed completely as it needs a supply of oxygen. Also, elicit that everything in the furnace is likely to burn up, even the Salt family, leaving only ash. This would be an irreversible change.

Trick candle demo

Light the tealight again. Leave it burning so you have a pool of liquid wax at the base of the wick.

At the same time, light the trick candle. Choose a child and sing Happy Birthday to them and prompt them to blow out the candle. The candle will relight. Repeat this a few times, just for fun. Act surprised that it won't go out. They'll soon tell you that it's a special candle.

Return to the tealight. Note that the liquid wax pool is reducing. Ask where the wax has gone. (There is more about this in the catching alight demo in *Kensuke's Kingdom* on p. 140.) Explain that the liquid wax taps up the wick and is heated so it becomes wax vapour. It is this wax vapour that burns when the candle is alight.

Ask them what is making the trick candle relight. They will notice the sparks. In the wick, there are tiny pieces of magnesium that spark to relight the small amount of wax vapour that remains around the hot wick. Reinforce that it is the wax vapour that is the fuel for the candle and that the wax is changed into other gases that are lost. The process is irreversible.

Floating wish paper demo

Do the demo as described in *The Northern Lights* chapter (p. 176).

Set up and light the wish paper on a plate and watch the ash float into the air. Discuss how the hot gases are rising and they carry the lightweight ashes with them. Note again that the gases made by the burning process are lost to the air and the process cannot be reversed.

 ## Finale

Now is the perfect moment to go out and toast marshmallows on a fire (being aware of those who cannot eat egg or gelatine for dietary or religious reasons) to celebrate all the sweet related science you have done. If you have a firepit area in school and have a qualified adult to lead the activity, go out and toast marshmallows on long kebab sticks. Keep pointing out that some changes are reversible (the marshmallow melts) but some are irreversible (the marshmallow toasts or burns). You could even read the rest of the book as you sit around the fire.

 ## Teacher's top tips

As with all demos, practise them before the lesson so you know you can make them work safely with the children in the room.

Work pretty fast, talking all the time. It's the discussion that is key here and you don't want any pregnant pauses while you rummage for equipment, so lay it all out before you start. Treat it like a performance.

Be aware that you may have to fill in a risk assessment and always work well back from the children, on a flame proof surface, to avoid any flames reaching them.

What next?

If you want to record your findings in a creative way then you could:

- Role-play: the Oompa Loompas meeting Veruca and her family in the furnace room and letting them out of the furnace. Have the Oompa Loompas explaining to the Salt family how the furnace works and why there is less left in the furnace after it has burned than there was before.

- Write a manual for the furnace room. Explain how the furnace requires fuel and the gases are released and escape out of the chimney. You could also give instructions on keeping the vents free from obstruction to allow oxygen in and keeping the chimney swept so the gases can escape.

- Write a letter of complaint from Mr Salt to Mr Wonka, complaining about the lack of safety in the nut room and how he and his precious daughter were nearly burned up in the furnace.

- Write a newspaper article about the event. You could have a science expert explaining how the furnace works and pointing out that, had the Salts gone into the furnace, it would have been irreversible!

- Write an Oompa Loompa poem about the Salt family ending up in the furnace and irreversibly combusting and becoming gases and ash – all because Veruca is so spoiled.

Assessing children's understanding

The following statements are indicators of basic understanding:

- Burning is a permanent/irreversible change.
- Burning paper makes ash, smoke and gases.
- You need a fuel and oxygen to burn something .

More advanced understanding:

- Burning is a chemical change; the oxygen combines with carbon and hydrogen in the fuel to become carbon dioxide and water vapour.
- When gases are lost into the air you cannot put them back and make the original material, so burning is an irreversible change.

Patterns they may be able to describe:

- If paper burns under a glass, the larger the glass, the longer it burns as there is more oxygen.

———————————————

5 *Kensuke's Kingdom*

Michael Morpurgo (1999)

TOPIC PLANNER

Story link	Science The water cycle	Activity	Page
What is a solid?	States of matter – ice Melting ice Observing	Flipping icebergs! (activity) Melting ice (demo/activity)	112–13
Water everywhere	Absorbent material Predicting	Choosing the best mop (investigation)	120
The football	Gas – another state of matter Observing and discussing	Using a gas to keep you afloat (demo/activity) Which gases are in air? (demo) Are the gases all the same? (demo)	123
Where did Kensuke get the water?	Rain catcher Designing and refining (tinkering)	Making a rain catcher (activity)	130
Rainy days	The water cycle Predicting Observing	Modelling the water cycle (activity) Collecting pure water from saltwater (demo)	133–4
Lighting the beacon	Burning wax Predicting Observing	Catching alight (demo)	139–40

Extra activities

This topic lends itself to outdoor activities. If you can combine it with an outdoor activity trip, a survival course or forest schools then you could include the following activities (under the proper supervision of trained adults and taking the relevant safety precautions, of course). All these things will bring the story to life and add to the magic and the engagement of the children.

- make bows from green wood;
- make arrows and spears by whittling wood;
- collect wood and tinder and build fires;
- climb trees;
- build shelters/camps;
- make hats to protect you from the sun;
- make maps and learn to use the points of the compass;
- make natural paints and brushes and paint in the Japanese style like Kensuke;
- try some shodo/calligraphy with your paint.

WHAT IS A SOLID?

Story link
The Peggy Sue sets sail.

THE SCIENCE 1: States of matter – ice

When you melt ice to liquid water you are not changing the matter – it is still water. You are, however changing the state of that matter. Water is unusual because as it changes state from liquid to solid, it expands. Most materials decrease in volume as they solidify, but not water: it increases in volume. To understand this fully, you'll need to be able to picture what is going on with the molecules of water.

The smallest part of water you can get is a molecule of water. In a liquid, these molecules are attracted to one another so that the molecules stay attached to one another. These are loose bonds that allow the molecules to move around, slide over one another and swap places so the liquid can change shape to fit the container it is in.

However, in solid water, the molecules are more spread out and fixed in place by strong bonds. These bonds do not allow the molecules to move so they remain fixed into a shape and will keep that shape, regardless of the container it is in.

As the molecules of solid water are held further apart in the solid, the solid is less dense than the liquid. It takes up a greater volume than the same amount of liquid water does, so it is light for its size (less dense) compared with liquid water.

As explained in the chapter *The Northern Lights* (p. 155), less dense materials will float on more dense materials, so ice will float in liquid water.

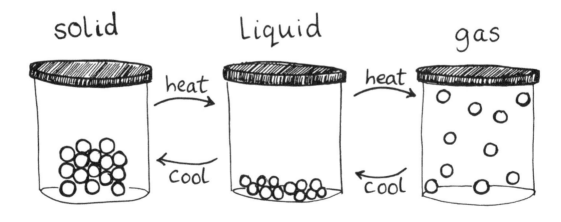

ACTIVITY 1: Flipping icebergs!

You will need:

- margarine tubs full of water – frozen to make huge ice cubes (icebergs)
- large clear tanks/storage boxes of water, at about room temperature
- videos of real icebergs turning over.

 ## Storify the science

Read Chapter 1. Ask the children what they would be worried about if they were embarking on a long journey around the world by boat. Grandma warns them about icebergs but why are icebergs so dangerous to sailors?

Now set the challenge as laid out in the section below.

While the children are watching their iceberg, talk about how much of the ice cube is underwater. They will notice that about 90 per cent of it is underwater. The ice floats in the water (but is not so buoyant that it sits on top of the water). Ice floats because water has a special property – it increases in volume as it becomes solid ice as the molecules are further apart when bonded as a solid than they are when they are a liquid.

As time passes, they may notice that the ice below the surface is melting faster than the ice above the surface and the shape is changing from a cube to a mushroom-like shape, with a large top and a narrower section below.

Talk about solid water (ice) and liquid water. Explain that melting is a change in state. The liquid and the solid are both water. It can be frozen back to ice or melted to water. Only the state has changed. The words solid and liquid are names of states of matter.

You could draw diagrams (if you can manage it without jogging the tanks) of the two different states of water (see facing page).

Ask the children what they think will happen. Accept all their answers, without correcting them or giving away the answer.

Eventually, the iceberg should tip over – the melting of the ice below the surface makes the iceberg top heavy and it should tip over. Once the heavier part is at the bottom, it will be more stable because the centre of gravity is lower. (See p. 207 for information about the centre of gravity.)

This happens with real icebergs – you can find videos of it on the internet to show them. Just search for 'iceberg flipping over'.

Set the challenge

Fill your tank to about 10 cm deep with water and put your iceberg into the water.

Does it float or sink?

How much of the ice cube is under the water?

Can you identify the different states of water?

Watch closely – what happens?

 # Teacher's top tips

This process takes time. It may be 20 minutes before the icebergs tip over, although, if you jog the table, it will be quicker! It can be a real wow moment if you let them predict what will happen but don't tell them the answer so they can look for evidence that their idea is correct.

You'll want to keep them busy while they watch so you can do some teacher led talk from the front as explained above or you could ask them to draw what they see in detail, using art materials. However, take care to keep the tables as still as possible as even a small wave can easily tip an iceberg and you'll want the children to see that an iceberg can flip without the assistance of a wave.

Don't show them the videos of icebergs first – let the first flip of their iceberg be a surprise.

Make sure that they understand that ice and water are the same material in different states.

While the iceberg is a great starting point, don't forget to teach them that the molecules in a solid are strongly bonded and the shape of a solid won't change (unless a force is applied to it). Their icebergs are changing shape because they are melting and becoming a liquid.

Once the icebergs have flipped, you may want to point out to the children that both the warm air and the water will melt the ice but the water in the tank will transfer its heat faster than the air. This is why the submerged part melts first.

What results should I expect?

As the shape of the iceberg changes, it will become unstable, with a high centre of gravity and they should flip over after about 20 minutes.

 # Finale

Play a game of 'Odd One Out'. Show the children these three items:

- transparent bottle of water (lid on)
- transparent bottle of sugar (lid on)
- large plastic cube (or ice cube).

Ask the children to suggest which is the odd one out of these three objects. Any answer is acceptable as long as it is justified. This activity really gets them talking and using scientific vocabulary. Allow time to share an idea with a partner and then ask for ideas to share with the class.

They might say the odd one out is:

- the water because it is a liquid;
- the cube because you can't pour it;
- the cube because it is red;
- the cube because it isn't in a bottle.

Accept all justified answers. Listen out for any misconceptions such as the sugar being a liquid because you can 'pour it'. Show them the sugar using a hand-held digital microscope to see the individual crystals and compare this to a drop of water. It is easy to see, at close inspection, that the sugar is made of tiny solids.

Encourage the correct use of the words 'solid' and 'liquid'.

 THE SCIENCE 2: Melting ice

When you melt a solid to a liquid you are changing the state of that substance. You can melt a solid by heating it above its melting point, which gives the molecules in the solid more energy and they start to move around (vibrate) more. As the solid warms, the molecules have sufficient energy to break the bonds that hold them in place and the solid becomes a liquid with looser bonds that allow the molecules to move around one another.

But there are ways to mess with the way this process works.

When snow is forecast, the roads are 'gritted' with a mixture of sand and salt. But why?

When salt (sodium chloride) is dissolved in water it is broken up into sodium ions and chloride ions. These ions are present in the salty water, even though we cannot see them. In order to freeze, the molecules of water must bond back together to make their solid structure but the sodium ions and chloride ions in the saltwater prevent this from happening. It is harder for salty water to freeze so it remains as a liquid at lower temperatures.

If you sprinkle salt onto an ice cube, the salt will dissolve in the thin layer of water at the surface (where the ice has melted) and makes liquid saltwater. This process continues as the salt comes into contact with the ice underneath, making more salty water that is a liquid even at this low temperature.

Of course, if it is cold enough, even salty water will freeze but the saltier the water, the lower the freezing point so a good sprinkle of salt on the road can make salty water that remains as a liquid in temperatures well below 0 °C.

Many of the icebergs in our oceans were formed from freshwater glaciers. Some are formed from salty sea ice.

DEMO/ACTIVITY 2: Melting ice cubes

You will need:

- hot water at about 70 °C (for adult use only)
- a hairdryer (safety checked for use at your establishment – for adult use only)
- two clear glasses/pots
- ice cubes (enough for two per pair of children plus two for the demo)
- saucers (enough for one per ice cube)
- salt

 Storify the science

Ask the children to recall the iceberg flipping from the last lesson. Ask them why the ice melted. They should be able to tell you that the water was warmer than the ice so it melted the ice. They may also be able to tell you that the warm air will also melt the ice but that the water transfers its heat faster.

Melting ice cubes demo

At a safe distance from the children do the following demonstrations:

- Put an ice cube in a large (pint-sized), clear glass of hot (70 °C) water. Watch how fast it melts.
- Again, at a safe distance from the children, put an ice cube in an empty clear glass or pot and warm it with a hairdryer on the medium setting (not the hot setting as you'll hurt your hand if you're steadying the glass). Watch how fast it melts.

You could race the hairdryer against the hot water. Hold the hairdryer back from the glass to avoid splashing any water out and onto the hairdryer.

The hot water will melt the ice very quickly. The hot air will melt the ice but it will take longer. Relate this to the iceberg melting faster below the waterline.

Ask them what people do when there is ice or snow on the car or on the roads/pavements. Ask if they use a hairdryer! Elicit that people might use the heater in the car or hot water to melt the ice in their windscreens and put down sand, salt or grit on a salty pavement.

Explain that we are going to observe what happens when you salt an icy road.

Set the challenge

You are going to observe two ice cubes melting. Sprinkle one of your ice cubes with a teaspoon of salt. Try to sprinkle the salt mostly over one end of the ice cube. Don't get any salt on your other ice cube.

Now watch carefully. Compare the salted ice cube to the unsalted ice cube all the time.

As you watch, think about these questions:

- What might happen?
- Which one might melt first?
- Do they melt in the same way?
- Do they move or stay still?

 # Teacher's top tips

You'll probably want to make your own ice cubes for this so you can make them all the same shape and size. Ice cube bags create ice cubes with rounded bottoms that can be fairly regular if you store them flat as they freeze, but ice cube trays create the most regular shapes.

Melting the ice cubes takes a little time, maybe even as much as 20 minutes. However, the changes are rapid enough to keep the children engaged, particularly at the start. You may want to get them to draw the ice cubes every two minutes (or take photos if you can afford the printer ink). This will keep them busy and focussed on the ice cubes.

The more observant children will notice that the salt looks wet almost immediately after it is sprinkled onto the ice cube. Even where the salt is heaped up, the water is absorbed up into the salt so that all of it is wet.

If they can observe the ice without jogging it, they will also see it swivel as it melts as one part may melt more quickly than another, causing it to become unstable and move to a more a balanced position (see explanation of centre of gravity p. 207 in the Alice chapter). This will only happen if you sprinkle one end of the ice cube with salt rather than evenly all over the ice cube.

You could stop once you are satisfied the children have seen the difference in the way the ice cubes melt. You could just leave the saucers on the table while you move on to another activity so they can keep half an eye on them.

You may want to investigate whether it makes a difference if you add different amounts of salt. You could change the amount of salt and time how long it takes to melt. Try it out at home first so you know that you can get different results from your particular ice cubes with different amounts of salt. You'll also need to check that your ice cubes aren't so huge that it takes hours to melt them completely, as your children will lose focus if it takes longer than 20 minutes or so.

What results should I expect?

The salted ice cubes will melt very differently to the unsalted ones. The salt will tend to create grooves in the ice cube that melt into crevasses, leaving tiny shards of ice cube standing. The unsalted ones will tend to stay much the same shape and just decrease in size.

The salted ice cube melts more quickly.

 Finale

You can make ice cream using salty water!

You will need:

- ice (four cups)
- salt (half a cup)
- large sealed tub
- small food bags
- ice cream mix

Find a recipe for a basic ice cream mix; most involve some double cream, sugar and vanilla. This works quite well:

- one cup of double cream (straight from the fridge)
- one tbsp caster sugar
- one tsp vanilla essence

Mix up the ice cream ingredients and put them into a small sandwich bag, sealing it carefully. You may want to double bag it!

Then, put the bag of ice cream mix into a sealed tub of ice cubes and salt. Put on some oven gloves (as it gets really cold) and shake the tub, moving the salty slush around the bag of ice cream mix. After a little while, your ice cream mix will begin to solidify.

You can compare whether it works as well with just ice (no salt).

The salted ice will drop to a much colder temperature than just ice. The warmer ice cream mix will lose heat to the ice and cause the salted ice to melt, thereby freezing the ice cream. The ice alone won't drop to a temperature low enough to effectively freeze the ice cream.

 What next?

If you want to record your findings in a creative way then you could:

- Write a letter to Grandma about the day you saw the iceberg flip over. Explain how the solid ice melts to liquid water and this happens faster to the part that is submerged. Then the floating iceberg becomes unstable and tips over. Reassure Grandma that you're all OK and that you are very good at spotting icebergs and will stay well clear as 90 per cent is hidden under the water.

- Write a new chapter or a page in the 'Ship's Log', recounting the time you saw an iceberg flip and explaining everything you know about icebergs from the encyclopaedia. Make sure you use the terms 'solid' and 'liquid'.

- Draw a series of annotated diagrams to go in the 'Ship's Log' about icebergs and why they flip over. Make sure you label the solid and liquid parts.

- Write a page for a traveller's recipe book, explaining how to make ice cream without a freezer, using salt and ice.

- Role-play: being Michael waking up on a frosty morning. Explain to your parents why it's a good idea to sprinkle salt on the deck.

 ## Assessing children's understanding

The following statements are indicators of basic understanding:

- You can change water to ice by freezing and back again by warming. This is called a change in state.

- Icebergs float in water but only about 10 per cent of the iceberg shows above the water.

- Icebergs tip over when the bottom melts away and the top is now the heaviest part. It is unstable when it is top-heavy.

- Adding salt made the ice cube melt faster.

More advanced understanding:

- When you heat ice, you give the molecules energy and they start to move more. The strong bonds between molecules of solid ice are broken and the solid becomes a liquid with weaker bonds between the molecules.

- Icebergs float in water because ice is less dense than water. This is because the strong bonds that make the water into a solid push the molecules further apart than they are in liquid water.

- Icebergs tip over when the lower part melts because they become unstable – the centre of gravity is too high to balance in that position. Flipping over lowers the centre of gravity and makes it stable again.

- The lower part of the ice in our experiment melts faster because it is in contact with warmer water rather than air and the heat can transfer more quickly from the water than the air.

- Saltwater freezes at a lower temperature than water so if you add salt to ice, it dissolves in the layer of water at the surface and makes the rest of the ice cube melt more quickly.

Patterns they may be able to describe:

- The more salt you add, the faster the ice cube melts.

WATER EVERYWHERE

Story link
The journey begins.

THE SCIENCE: Absorbent material

Some materials absorb liquids by drawing the moisture up into the fabric. This is capillary action as explained with the paper flower investigation in the *Alice's Adventures in Wonderland* chapter (p. 212).

Different fabrics contain different fibres and different spaces between the fibres. It is the space inside the fibres and between the fibres that matters. If there are very small spaces, then water molecules will be drawn in by capillary action. It doesn't happen if the spaces are too large.

In order to mop up something really efficiently, you'll need a material that absorbs water well.

INVESTIGATION: Choosing the best mop

You will need:

- a selection of different materials that might have been available on the boat. Include cotton sheet, dish cloth, sugar paper, newspaper, writing paper, kitchen towel, sponge or foam if you can get

thin strips of it (all pre-cut into 2 cm wide strips if you want to save time)
- pots or tanks to hold the water
- rulers
- sellotape

Storify the science

Read the start of Chapter 2. Ask the children to imagine life on board a boat. Michael describes the boat as wet and says 'to be dry again was a real luxury'.

Talk about the things that could get wet and make life uncomfortable, such as socks or bedding.

Imagine life on board and keeping things tidy and dry. Michael talks about the jobs he had to do such as mopping up.

Some fabrics are good for mopping up spills. If you spill something on the floor, what might you use to mop it up?

Introduce the idea that we are going to test different fabrics to see how useful they are for mopping up spills.

Set the challenge

You are going to test which fabric will absorb the most water.

Before you begin, decide which one you think will absorb the most water and give a reason for your prediction.

Now collect up strips of the materials you want to test. You are going to arrange them so that each strip hangs down from a ruler. You are going to dip one end in some water and measure how far up the strip the water will go. It might look like this:

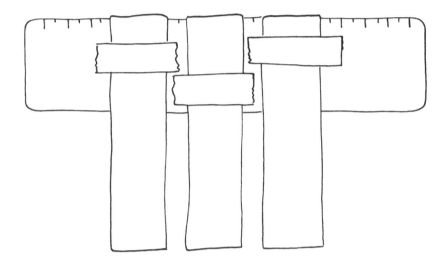

Now think about how to make your test fair. You'll need to consider:

*   the width of each strip;
*   the length of each strip;
*   the depth of the water;
*   how long you leave the strips in the water;
*   what you will measure.

Once you have worked out how to carry out the test fairly and what you will measure, carry out your test and gather evidence to prove which material absorbs the most water.

Was your prediction correct?

 ## Teacher's top tips

Spend time at the end of the lesson reviewing the children's predictions in light of the results.

You could look at the fibres and how well the water absorbs with a hand held digital microscope as described in the finale of the paper flowers investigation in the *Alice's Adventures in Wonderland* chapter (see p. 212).

If your children are independent and organised, you could let them cut their own strips of materials but as scissors in schools are often made for paper only, you may want to cut at least the tougher fabric for them, with a decent pair of fabric scissors.

They can do all the tests at once if they dangle all the strips from the same ruler into the same pot.

Sticking the paper to the ruler then cutting them all so that they are all just long enough to touch the base of an empty pot can be easier than cutting them first and then finding they're not long enough to reach the water!

Provide newspaper for the table so they can lay the wet strips down to measure how far up the water has risen more easily.

You could also use this data in your maths lesson if you want to draw bar charts of the data to present your findings.

It would be hard to find space to store rubbish on the boat so you may want to discuss which one is best for use on board bearing this in mind. You could even dry the strips on a washing line and see which ones are suitable for re-use.

What results should I expect?

Sugar paper, newspaper and kitchen towel will absorb the water well. You may also find one of the cloths will absorb well too.

 ## What next?

If you want to record your findings in a creative way then you could:

- Write a review of the different papers and fabrics, for a sailing magazine, recommending which one would be the best to keep the deck dry.
- Role-play: being the family at the market. Choose items to buy for drying the deck. Discuss all the considerations such as storage when wet, reusability, and absorption.
- Design a mop for use on a sailing boat. Draw your design and write an advert for radio that explains why your mop is the best and how you tested the materials to find the most absorbent.

 ## Assessing children's understanding

The following statements are indicators of basic understanding:

- Certain papers and fabrics absorb more water than others. (The actual results will depend on what you test.)
- The water soaked up higher on the more absorbent papers or fabrics.

More advanced understanding:

- The water is absorbed into the spaces in and between the fibres by capillary action. The fibres and spaces between them must be tiny for this to happen.

———————————

THE FOOTBALL

Story link

Michael uses the football to stay afloat.

THE SCIENCE 1: Gas – another state of matter

Unlike solids and liquids, the molecules of a gas are free to roam. They are not constrained by bonds holding them to other like molecules, they can move around a space and occupy the entire volume inside a container.

In order to make liquid water into invisible water vapour gas, you must give it enough energy to wiggle and jiggle itself free of the bonds that hold it in a liquid until it has the energy to evaporate and reach the gaseous state.

Some materials exist as a gas at room temperature. Oxygen, nitrogen and carbon dioxide are all present as gases in the air, along with water vapour, in most places. While we are familiar with water as a liquid and a solid, we don't usually come across oxygen or nitrogen or carbon dioxide in a solid or liquid state. This is because they would need to be very cold (or compressed) in order to be a liquid and even colder to be a solid.

Gases spread out to fill the container. As they bump into the edges of the container, they exert a force upon it, pushing the sides outwards. This is why a football expands as you fill it with air.

As the molecules are very spread out, gases are not very dense. They are certainly less dense than water so a football filled with air has a low overall density because it is mostly air and it will float. You can find out more about density in the chapter *The Northern Lights* (see p. 155).

DEMO/ACTIVITY 1: Using a gas to keep you afloat

You will need:

- bottles of lemonade (or another transparent fizzy liquid – don't let it go flat before you start)
- a glass of water (adult use only)
- raisins
- tall transparent pots or glasses

Storify the science

Read Chapter 4 up to the point where Michael wakes up on the beach and realises his football is gone. Michael had held on to his football to stay afloat in the sea. Ask the children to imagine what that would be like. They may have experience of bobbing along in the swimming pool or the sea on an inflatable ball. Discuss how much of Michael would be in the water. Elicit that his body would be mostly in the water – his head and shoulders might be above the waterline but that would be all.

Ask the children to explain how the ball kept Michael afloat. Listen to their explanations and accept all answers without indicating whether they are right or wrong.

Open the lemonade.

Pour some lemonade out into the pots and ask the children to observe the lemonade. Ask them what they can see. The bubbles will form and rise to the top of the lemonade and pop. This won't be surprising for them but it's good to note that the bubbles themselves rise to the top.

Show them a raisin. Ask them if they think it will float. Accept their answers without revealing anything. Drop it into the water. It will sink to the bottom. This may be surprising as a common misconception is that small, light objects will float while heavy ones sink.

Next give them each a raisin and ask them to drop it in their lemonade and watch. The raisin will collect bubbles all over it and rise to the top where the bubbles pop and the raisin sinks again.

Discuss how this relates to the football. Without the football (and the bubble of air inside) Michael might sink to the bottom too.

Explain that the molecules in gas are very spread out, much more spread out than the molecules in the water. We can say that the bubbles of gas are less dense than the water. If there are enough bubbles, the overall density of the raisin and bubbles is less dense than the water and it floats. Without the air bubbles, the raisin is more dense than the water and it sinks. This may be beyond the comprehension of some but worth saying for those that are able to follow the logic.

 Teacher's top tips

Make sure your pots are transparent and as clean as possible – dirt in the pots will make the bubbles form too quickly and the lemonade may go flat.

Check your lemonade variety is fizzy enough in advance and use the raisins you plan to use in the lesson. If the lemonade is flat, it won't work.

You could put the raisins directly into the bottle if you take the label off the bottle so the children can see inside.

THE SCIENCE 2: Gases in the air

There are many different gases in the air. It contains approximately:

- 78 per cent nitrogen
- 21 per cent oxygen
- 1 per cent argon
- 0.04 per cent carbon dioxide
- 0.4 per cent water vapour.

In order to burn anything you need a fuel (in this case the candle wax) and oxygen. If the fuel runs out or the oxygen runs out, the flame will go out.

It is hard to imagine because we can't see it, but air molecules fill the space around us and are moving around all the time, bumping into us and the other objects and exerting a force on everything they meet. We call this air pressure.

The air around us is at a certain pressure. If you go up a mountain, the air pressure is less because the air molecules are more spread out (less dense). If you remove air from a bottle, by sucking it out, you lower the pressure inside the bottle by taking some of the gas molecules away. The remaining air in the bottle is now at a lower pressure because there are fewer molecules to fill the space. At this point, the sides of the bottle are likely to collapse in on themselves as the air pressure outside the bottle is greater than inside and pushes inwards more powerfully than the air inside pushes outwards.

In this demo, a burning candle is placed inside an upturned glass in a dish of water. As the flame gradually goes out, water moves into the glass. There are many factors at play here and, as often happens, scientists don't agree in their theories about exactly what is going on but the main events can be described as follows:

The oxygen inside a glass is used by a burning a candle, and carbon dioxide is produced. The candle heats the air inside the glass, causing it to expand so that some of the air bubbles out. Then the flame goes out as the oxygen is used up, and the air cools. The air pressure outside the glass is now greater than the pressure inside the glass. The air on the outside will be pressing in on that glass. The glass is too strong to collapse so instead, water around the bottom of the glass is pushed in by the air outside the glass until the air pressure inside the glass is back to the same as that outside and the water stops entering the glass.

DEMO 2: Which gases are in the air?

You will need:

- a tealight candle
- a tall narrow glass container such as a drinking glass (for adult use only)
- a plate/shallow bowl (with a lip to stop the water spilling off)
- coloured water
- matches.

 ## Storify the science

Read the rest of Chapter 4, from the point where Michael wakes up on the beach to his first night in the cave and his attempt to make fire. Ask the children what you need to make a fire. Elicit that you need something to burn and a flame. They may also tell you oxygen. Accept all answers and carry out the following demo without indicating which answers are correct.

Place the plate/shallow bowl where they can all see it and fill it with coloured water up to 1 or 2 cm deep. Place a tealight (or candle that will stand up by itself) in the centre of the liquid. Show them the glass and ask what will happen if you put the glass over the candle. Accept all answers without indicating that any are correct.

Place the glass over the candle and watch. The candle will burn for a short while and then go out. Then the coloured water rises up inside the glass. If you use a tealight, it will float on the liquid. Ask them what happened.

It's fun to repeat this a few times as it's quick and easy to do and gets a good reaction. Ask the children why the water only rises a little way up the glass each time. Once the children have had a chance to offer their own ideas lead them to the following explanation:

In order to burn the wax, you need oxygen. Once the oxygen in the jar has been used up, the flame goes out. When the flame goes out, the air cools and the gas inside the jar is now at a lower pressure than the outside air. The outside air pressure pushes the water into the glass to equalise the pressure.

Note that the flame does not last very long in the glass as there is not much oxygen in the air – only about 21 per cent. The rest is made up of other gases.

Take time to marvel at the fact that, although we don't notice it, air is pushing on us in all directions, all the time. We can see that the force is quite strong because it pushes the water upwards, against gravity.

 ## Teacher's top tips

Place a match stick under the lip of the glass (making sure the water level still covers the bottom of the glass) to ensure there is enough space for the coloured water to enter the glass.

If you search for videos of 'storage tank implosions' or 'soft drink can implosions' on the internet, you can see exactly how powerful air pressure can be. At the time of writing, The Sci Guys have a good video on their YouTube channel.

 ## THE SCIENCE 3: Carbon dioxide

You can make carbon dioxide by mixing bicarbonate of soda with an acid such as vinegar. This causes a chemical reaction and the mixture bubbles up into a foam. Each bubble is full of carbon dioxide.

If you want to make this more exciting, you can add food colouring and a drop of washing up liquid. The addition of washing up liquid creates longer lasting foam.

Carbon dioxide is not required for a flame to burn which is why it is used in some fire extinguishers to smother a flame by filling the area around the flame with carbon dioxide to exclude the oxygen and put out the flame.

It is also a more dense gas than the other constituents of air so, if you make bubbles of carbon dioxide in a tall container, once the bubbles pop, the carbon dioxide will tend to stay in the container rather than float out into the air. This makes it fun to play with and you can pour it!

 ## DEMO 3: Are the gases all the same?

There's a nice demo in the *Charlie and the Chocolate Factory* chapter, in the section called 'Making fizz' that works brilliantly here too. You can find it on p. 94.

It will lead you through the process of making carbon dioxide and using it to put out matches and candles.

The children are usually amazed that a gas can be poured. You can explain that this gas is more dense than the other gases in the air, so it sinks. That's why it stayed in the jug and didn't escape into the room. Discuss with them how you can see evidence that gases are present even if you can't see the gas itself.

What next?

If you want to record your findings in a creative way then you could:

- Investigate steam boats to see how gases (in this case water vapour) can be used to power an engine.
- Role-play a conversation between Michael and his father about why the football floats in the water.
- Draw a design for a fire extinguisher for the boat that uses vinegar and bicarbonate of soda to make carbon dioxide to put out the flames. Annotate your drawing to explain how it works.

Assessing children's understanding

The following statements are indicators of basic understanding:

- The air is made of gases. It is made up of oxygen and nitrogen, hydrogen and carbon dioxide and a little bit of water vapour.
- Molecules of gas are very spread out and moving all the time.
- Bubbles of gas will rise to the surface of water.
- You can make water into a gas by heating it.
- You can make bubbles of carbon dioxide by mixing bicarbonate of soda and vinegar.
- Different gases have different properties. Carbon dioxide sinks in air. Oxygen is needed to burn a fuel.

More advanced understanding:

- Gas is less dense than water so bubbles float and rise to the surface.
- Molecules of gas are not bonded to each other as they are in liquids and solids. They have lots of energy to move around the space they are in and the bump into objects (including ourselves) and exert a force on them.
- When you remove gas from a container you lower the pressure inside the vessel.
- Air pressure will push in on a container that has a lower pressure inside it than outside. This may collapse the walls of the container.

WHERE DID KENSUKE GET THE WATER?

Story link

Kensuke provides water for Michael.

THE SCIENCE: Rain catcher

In order to make a decent rain catcher, the design should have a large surface area to catch as much rain as possible and be made from something waterproof so it won't leak. Ideally it will have a spout for drinking from too.

It's as simple as that!

The main focus of this activity is focussed on selecting the right materials (so make sure you provide some useless ones for them to avoid) and about tinkering with a design to make it work.

ACTIVITY: Making a rain catcher

You will need to assemble a pack of materials for each group that is identical. It should include resources Kensuke might have had from the shipwreck:

- A4 sized piece of paper
- A4 sized piece of foil
- A4 sized piece of plastic bag or clingfilm
- a short length of sellotape/masking tape (30 cm)
- A4 sized piece of sheet/cotton cloth
- any other items you can provide for all that will offer some help in constructing a water catcher or items that will be useless and should be avoided.
- a watering can
- a large tray.

Storify the science

Revisit the part of Chapter 4 where Michael considers drinking brackish water from a rock pool. Ask the children what it feels like to swallow sea water. Some children may have experienced how sick it can make you feel.

Now read Chapter 5 up to the point where Michael tells how he searched his own end of the island for fresh running water but found none. Ask the children where they think Kensuke gets his water from. They may answer that there must be a stream on Kensuke's end of the island but if there is no stream how could he get clean water? Accept all answers and lead them to the idea that he could collect rainwater.

Ask what Kensuke might use to catch the rain. Introduce the idea that they are going to make rain catchers. Draw an island on one end of your whiteboard. At the other draw a rain cloud. Tell them they have until the rain cloud reaches the island to make something to catch the rain.

While they are busy making, rub out the cloud and redraw it a little closer to the island. When you can see they are nearly ready, move the cloud over to the island and get ready to test their contraptions.

 ## Set the challenge

You are going to make something to catch the rain. Kensuke would have had limited resources and so will you. You must only use the items in your pack so plan what you will make before you start.

- You must catch as much rain as possible.
- You must be able to stand your contraption on the sand to gather rain.
- It should be possible to drink the rain from your contraption.

When you design your rain catcher think about:

- which materials to use;
- what to do first;
- how to avoid making accidental holes in the materials.

 ## Teacher's top tips

Encourage the children to think ahead and to solve problems as they meet them.

Stick lengths of tape to the edge of their table so they can see how much they have used and what is left.

When you are ready to test, put each contraption on the tray and pour a little water over it, using a watering can so it looks like rain. Look out for collapsing sides and leaks. If it collects some rain then give them some points. If it keeps the water in without leaking, award more. And award maximum points if it does both of these and it would be possible to drink from it.

What results should I expect?

One of the most successful designs is a simple foil tray, like a take-away container. It has a large surface area and is fully waterproof. But they will make all kinds of mad designs and you'll need to test and appreciate all of them!

What next?

If you want to record your findings in a creative way then you could:

- Write an extra chapter for the book (or an entry in the Ship's Log) about your attempt to make a rain catcher. Explain what you made and whether it worked. You could also draw a design for one you plan to make the next day that would be more successful, based on what you learned today.
- Write a leaflet that could be part of a survival kit stored in lifeboats, giving basic instructions on how to make a rain catcher. You could even make the kit to go with it.
- Role-play: telling Kensuke about your rain catcher. You would need to demonstrate it as Kensuke didn't know many English words and Michael knew no Japanese at this point in the story.

Assessing children's understanding

The following statements are indicators of basic understanding:

- The foil is a better material to use because it is waterproof.
- If you want to use the paper, you need to cover it with plastic so it won't go soggy in the rain.
- My design was good because . . .
- My design didn't work because . . .

More advanced understanding:

- The rain catcher needed to have the maximum surface area possible to catch more rain.
- I chose to use this material because I knew that . . .

RAINY DAYS

Story link

Kensuke provides water.

THE SCIENCE 1: The water cycle

The water on Earth is the same water that has always been here, since the beginnings of the Earth.

It can exist in three states on the Earth because it is not too hot and not too cold. Just like Goldilocks' porridge, the Earth is just the right temperature. It is not too close to the Sun where all the water would be a gas and not so far away that the water is permanently frozen.

When liquid water is heated, the molecules are given enough energy to break free from their loose bonds and to become an invisible gas called water vapour. This process is called evaporation. The molecules spread out to fill the available space and have enough energy to move about as a gas.

If you cool water vapour it will return to its liquid state. This is called condensation.

Condensation and evaporation are reversible and are the processes by which substances change in state.

The breath we exhale is full of water vapour from our lungs as the internal surfaces of our lungs are wet so lots of this moisture ends up in our breath. If you breathe onto a cool surface, such as a glass mirror, you can see the liquid water form on the surface. We often refer to these tiny droplets of water as condensation as it is the process of condensation that has caused them to form there.

If you breathe out on a frosty day, you can see clouds of droplets in the air. Again these droplets are formed by condensation. The water vapour in our breath cools to form liquid water as it hits the cold air. The droplets are so tiny that they can remain suspended in the air like a cloud. Children often think this visible cloud is water vapour but water in its gaseous state is invisible so it is worth pointing out that if we can see a cloud then it's liquid water droplets we can see.

You can see a cloud of condensation form above the spout of a boiling kettle as the invisible water vapour hits the cooler air, above the kettle, and condenses to form a cloud of visible, liquid water droplets, suspended in the air.

The water in the seas (and other large bodies of water) is constantly evaporating. The Sun's heat energy and the movement energy of the wind give the top layer of liquid water enough energy to escape the bonds that hold it in a liquid and the molecules become a gas. The water does not have to boil for evaporation to occur; as long as the very uppermost molecules have enough energy to break free from their bonds, evaporation will happen.

When these molecules of invisible water vapour gas meet the cold air, higher in the sky, they condense back to a liquid, forming tiny droplets in the air that we can see as a cloud. The cloud will eventually rain on the Earth and the water molecules begin their journey back to the sea again.

Evaporation and condensation are key processes in this water cycle. The children need to experience these processes to help them understand the following water cycle model.

 ## ACTIVITY 1: Modelling the water cycle

You will need:

- a large clear plastic box or tank
- frozen ice pack
- clingfilm
- warm water (40° C maximum for safety)
- transparent plastic pots

- ice cubes
- iced water
- a glass (adult use only)
- mirrors (child-safe and chilled).

 ## Storify the science

Before you read, set a glass on the table. Now fill it with iced water – the more ice the better. Observe as condensation forms on the outside of the glass. They may tell you the glass has leaked. You can challenge this misconception by holding the glass over your head and asking whether the glass really will leak on you.

You could also give out mirrors and let the children breathe on them. This works well if you put the bag of mirrors in the fridge before you start to ensure they are good and cold. Discuss where this wetness on the glass has come from. Lead them to the idea that there is water vapour in the air and in our breath.

Put a droplet of clean water on the back of each child's hand for them to observe and then begin to read to them.

(They should notice that it dries up. They may tell you that the droplet sank into their skin. This is a common misconception. Only the dead skin cells on the surface absorb a little water otherwise we would all swell up in the rain. Lead them to the idea that the water has evaporated and is now in the air as water vapour.)

Meanwhile, read the first few pages of Chapter 10, to the point where the rain stops. Ask the children where the rain comes from. Listen to their ideas. Some children may know that the rain is part of the water cycle. Others may have never thought to ask where clouds come from.

Explain that you are going to make some rain.

Set up the clear plastic tank in the front of the class and give out the clear plastic pots.

Pour a little of the warm water into the bottom of the pots and pour some into your tank.

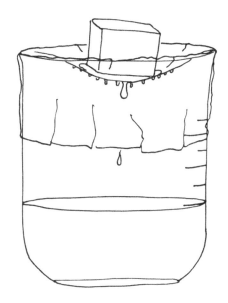

Give them each a piece of clingfilm and ask them to cover their pots as you cover your tank at the front, sealing the clingfilm over the edges of the tank and pressing it down. Ask them what they notice. The inside of their pots, and your tank, should begin to mist up with condensation.

Now, place an ice cube on top of each pot, in the centre of the clingfilm. You may need to make a little dent in the top as the clingfilm tends to dome as the warm water makes the air in the pot expand a little. Put the frozen ice pack on your tank. Now watch carefully.

Within a few minutes, a droplet of water will condense below the ice cube and gather at the lowest point on the clingfilm. When the droplet is large enough, it will fall down. And there you have your rain!

As you watch this process with the children, talk all the time about the warm water evaporating into water vapour. This water vapour condenses on the cold surfaces and will eventually fall back down to the warm water, like rain.

Make the point that this is a closed system, just like the Earth. The water from the sea evaporates into invisible water vapour and condenses as clouds. The rain falls back to the ground and may form rivers or go directly back into the sea.

 ## Teacher's top tips

Try out the equipment before the lesson – some clingfilm is not very clingy and won't make a good seal around the pot. It is worth investing in a decent brand for this lesson.

The children may think that the moisture from the melting ice cube is dripping through the clingfilm. To demonstrate that the clingfilm is waterproof (and therefore, that the droplets on the inside of the pot are being formed by condensation of water vapour from the warm water) you can make a little bag of clingfilm, fill it with cold water and hold it up. Take care not to let any leak out of the edges and show them that water cannot pass through the cling film.

You could show them the video of 'The Children of the Water God' on Storytelling Schools' YouTube channel or read the story yourself from my other book *Science Through Storytelling* (Pottle and Smith, Hawthorn Press, 2015). The story explains the water cycle in the style of a Greek myth and there's a song to go with the story on YouTube too!

THE SCIENCE 2: Evaporation from salty water

When salty water dries up, it is only the water molecules that evaporate. Any salt in the water is left behind. This is why we feel a crust of salt left on our faces after a day at the beach – the water evaporates, leaving the salt behind.

 DEMO 2: Collecting pure water from saltwater

You will need:

- clear plastic boxes or tanks (one per group)
- water
- food colouring

- salt
- clingfilm
- teacups or mugs
- ice packs (frozen)

 Storify the science

Return to the question of where Kensuke might be getting his water from. He could be gathering his water from the rain but ask the children to consider what he would do if it didn't rain for months on end. Ask the children if there is any way to use the seawater. They may suggest sieving it to remove the salt.

At this point, prepare some saltwater in a clean glass by mixing lots of salt with a glassful of drinking water. Dissolve the salt so the children can see the grains of salt 'disappearing' into solution.

Use a clean spoon to drip a single tiny droplet onto the back of the hand of a child with clean hands. You can do this for all the children present. Observe as the droplet evaporates. Let the children taste the salt left on their hands. Discuss what happened. Lead them to the idea that the water has evaporated leaving the salt behind.

Now prepare some warm saltwater (max 40 °C) in front of the children and add salt, stirring until it has dissolved. Discuss the fact that the water will now taste salty. Add food colouring and stir well.

Repeat the water cycle model as described in the previous activity, putting the water into a tank. This time put a cup or mug in the centre of the tank so that the edges sit above the level of the water and the cup does not fill up with coloured salty water but stays dry. You may need to stack one cup on another to stop them floating away or use a large mug. Now, put clingfilm over the top and put the ice pack on top, directly over the mug.

Ask the children what they think will happen. Encourage them to make predictions. Many will expect the liquid in the cup to be salty or coloured.

Leave this set up and go and do something else for a bit.

After half an hour, or so, there will be clean, fresh, uncoloured water dripping from the clingfilm into the cup.

Discuss how it is only the water that evaporates here. The salt and the colouring are left behind.

If you really want to finish with a flourish – let all the children have a taste of the water in the cup! Imagine how Kensuke might have achieved this on the island.

 ## Teacher's top tips

Make sure the cups are clean so you can taste the water safely.

If the children have washed their hands, they can dip a clean finger into the cup to taste so you only need a few spoonfuls of water for the whole class.

Look back at the predictions made by the children and see whether their ideas were supported by the evidence.

You only need a cool surface to condense the water – not ice. You can use a saucepan, with a glass lid, full of saltwater. Upturn the glass lid (the cool surface) and warm the pan of saltwater on a stove. If you place a cup under the centre of the unturned pan lid, the water vapour will condense on the lid and drip into the cup below. You may want to film this process for the children to see. It's not a suitable activity for most classrooms as you can't get that many children safely around a stove.

 ## What next?

You could:

- Role-play: Michael asking Kensuke where the rain comes from and Kensuke explaining with words and pictures, how the water cycle works;
- Draw posters explaining the water cycle – annotate each area to explain what is going on;
- Make a Powerpoint/website page version of the water cycle. Link extra pages to items on the page so that you can click on them to see the explanations of what is going on at each point;
- Write another survival leaflet explaining how to heat seawater and collect the condensation. Draw diagrams of the equipment and annotate them.

 ## Assessing children's understanding

The following statements are indicators of basic understanding:

- When you heat water it evaporates.
- When water vapour is cooled it condenses.
- You can evaporate pure water from seawater and the salt is left behind.

More advanced understanding:

- The water evaporated because it had enough energy to escape the loose bonds that hold it in a liquid.
- The water vapour gas condensed to liquid water on the ice pack/ice cube/glass lid because it was cold. The icepack/ice cube/cold lid cooled the molecules of water vapour and they slowed down and formed loose bonds and became a liquid.
- Evaporation and condensation are changes in state. Water vapour and liquid water are made from the same molecules but have different amounts of energy so they behave differently.

LIGHTING THE BEACON

Story link

Michael lights a beacon.

THE SCIENCE: Burning wax

Water is not the only substance that evaporates when it is given heat energy. When candles burn, it is the evaporated wax that is the fuel for the flame.

When you light a new candle, the wick will start to burn and go black. This burning is a permanent change. Then, the wax around the wick melts. **This melting is reversible**. If you blow the candle out, the molten wax will harden into a solid again.

Once the candle has reached the point where there is molten wax around the wick, this liquid wax is absorbed up the wick, where it is really warm, and the wax evaporates. This gaseous wax is now the fuel for the flame. **Burning the gas is an irreversible change**. As it burns, more liquid wax is tapped up the wick and evaporates, until all the wax is used up.

Children often think the wax has somehow melted away so watch out for this misconception and encourage them to notice that the candle gets smaller as the wax is burned.

 **DEMO: Catching alight**

You will need:

- small groups of children or a visualiser attached to a large screen so all the class can see!
- a new tealight for each demo
- a lighter.

 Storify the science

Read the latter part of Chapter 10, where Kensuke and Michael light the beacons to attract the attention of the passing boats. Ask the children what they know about lighting fires. Gather all the information they have. They may know a flame needs fuel and oxygen to burn. They may know ways to start a fire like Michael's fireglass or by rubbing sticks together.

Explain that you are going to look more closely at burning so they'll need to be in small groups.

Put a new tealight on the table, where they can all observe fairly closely (making sure hair is tied back and behaviour is calm). Ask the children to observe as you light it. Talk about the changes that occur straightaway. The wick goes black and the wax begins to melt. Ask which of these is reversible.

Ask the children about what is being burned. Is the wick actually burning away? What is getting used up by the flame? Help them to notice that the pool of wax is depleting. Lead them to the idea that the wax is what is burned away by the flame.

Then, with your lighter to hand, blow out the candle. Now bring the lighter close to the wick without touching. If you are fast enough, the flame will leap from lighter to wick while they are still a centimetre apart. Ask the children what happened. Repeat the process a few times so that all the children see it happen.

Go back to the idea that the wax is being burned by the flame. Yet the flame was nowhere near the pool of wax, at the base of the wick, when it jumped across. Lead them to the idea that the wax evaporates too and is present in the air around the wick where the flame is. For a short while after you blow out the flame, the wick remains warm and the wax continues to evaporate so the flame catches that gaseous wax alight, when it jumps.

Link this back to states of matter – we have evidence of wax in all three states here: solid wax, molten wax and invisible, gaseous wax that relights.

 Teacher's top tips

Make sure you follow any safety guidance and complete the relevant risk assessment when working with candles in your establishment.

As always, practise before the lesson!

The Royal Institution website has a great video of this happening so if it is not clear when you do the demo, follow it up with their close-up video so you can be sure all the children have seen it. If you search for 'candle trick' or 'flame jumping' you can find various videos of this.

What next?

If you want to record your findings in a creative way then you could:

- Video the process and allow the children to make voice-over tracks to accompany the video. If you use a video editing tool, such as iMovie, you can combine the audio with clips of video. You could slow the movie clip down to see the flame jump more clearly.
- Research fire-making methods (including Michael's fireglass method) and write a survival guide on ways to make fire. Make sure you include burning wax candles and explain how they work. Also provide safety information for your readers.
- Write another chapter where Kensuke's fire goes out and they have to make fire again. Include a candle in the story and a part where Kensuke shows Michael the jumping flame.

Assessing children's understanding

The following statements are indicators of basic understanding:

- Burning is an irreversible change.
- The wick went black when it burned and this is permanent.
- The candle wax melts. Any melted wax left when the flame is extinguished is cooled to a solid.
- Wax can be a gas too and it burns away.

More advanced understanding:

- Wax can exist in the three states: solid, liquid and gas, just like water.
- Liquid wax is tapped up the wick as a candle burns. The warmth of the wick evaporates the wax and it becomes a gas.
- The lighter flame can jump to the wick because it ignites the gas that is all around the wick.

6 *The Northern Lights*

Philip Pullman (1995)

He lifted out the first slide and dropped another into the frame. This was much darker; it was as if the moonlight had been filtered out. The horizon was still visible, with the dark shape of the hut and its light snow-covered roof standing out, but the complexity of the instruments was hidden in darkness. But the man had altogether changed: he was bathed in light, and a fountain of glowing particles seemed to be streaming from his upraised hand.

'That light', said the Chaplain, 'is it going up or coming down?'

'It's coming down', said Lord Asriel, 'but it isn't light. It's Dust.'

Something in the way he said it made Lyra imagine Dust with a capital letter, as if this wasn't ordinary dust.

(Pullman, 1995, pp. 21–2)

TOPIC PLANNER

Story link	Science Forces (through transport used on the journey)	Activity	Page
Falling and flying	Gravity and falling through air Balanced and unbalanced forces Testing against a control	Zeppelins (demo) Falling objects – autogyros (spinners) (investigation)	144–6
Canals and narrow boats – floating	Floating objects and upthrust Designing and testing (tinkering)	Making boats that are stable (activity)	155–6
Sledges – sliding	Friction Fair testing Recording results	Sledges and reducing the friction (investigation)	161–2

Story link	Science)	Activity	Page
Bear Feet – gripping	Friction Predicting Using the evidence to say whether prediction was correct	Bear feet and increasing the friction (investigation)	166
Broomsticks - streamlining	Air resistance Designing and testing (tinkering) Repeating a test to make sure it is repeatable.	Air resistance and streamlining – shaped for speed (investigation)	170
Hot air balloons – upthrust in the air	Density and upthrust Observing	Hot gases rising (demo 1 and 2)	175
Zeppelins and creating thrust	Thrust – a push force Designing and testing (tinkering)	Designing propellers (activity)	179–80

FALLING AND FLYING

> ### Story link
> The zeppelin floats.

THE SCIENCE: Gravity and falling through air – balanced and unbalanced forces

We are pulled towards the Earth by the force of gravity. Without it, we would float off into space. But how gravity works is a big puzzle even to the scientists that study it! So, what do we as teachers need to understand and what do we cover with the children?

The children need to know that:

- the force of gravity pulls us towards the centre of the Earth;

- gravity acts on us and everything around us including the air and the water in the sea!

- when you drop something, it is pulled downwards through air until it hits something that stops it falling. The air particles in its way slow the speed of the falling object. This slowing force is called air resistance;

- the shape of the object will affect the speed at which it falls – objects will fall more slowly if their shape has a larger surface area. More streamlined shapes will fall faster as the air particles are more likely to move past the object rather than bumping into the flat face of the object. There is less air resistance on a more streamlined shape;

- if an object is stationary (or moving at constant speed) there may be forces acting upon it that are equal in size but acting in opposite directions so the forces are balanced like a tug of war where both competitors pull with equal force;

- if an object is changing speed or starting to move then the opposing forces acting upon it are unbalanced like a tug of war when the stronger competitor is winning.

You may want to understand a little more about gravity and air resistance before you teach it. If so, read on.

First you need to know the difference between mass and weight:

Mass is a measurement of the amount of stuff there is in an object. Weight is a measurement of how heavy that mass is. Weight is dependent on gravity. The mass of an object is the same everywhere in the universe – a space helmet is made from the same amount of stuff wherever it is. However, that helmet feels heavier (weighs more) on Earth than on the moon because gravity is greater on the Earth.

A 100 g mass on Earth has weight of about 1 newton. When you hold that 100 g on your palm, you feel the downward force of that mass being pulled by the force of gravity. The size of that force is about 1 newton. If you held the same mass on the moon you would only feel a force of 0.2 newton. It weighs less on the moon as the moon is smaller and has less gravitational force.

Weight = mass x gravitational strength

Next, you need to know that everything with mass exerts a gravitational pull. It is odd to think of ourselves as having a gravitational pull on other objects and yet we do. Of course, it's a tiny force compared to the gravitational force of a planet but it is present nonetheless.

Every object that has mass attracts every other object that has mass. Larger masses exert a larger gravitational force. Each part of the mass exerts its own gravitational force so the larger the mass the larger the total gravitational force. So, a large mass such as the Earth has a much more significant gravitational force than a small mass such as a human body. If we jump up, we are pulled back down again by the gravitational pull of the Earth. The Earth is not pulled significantly towards us because we are tiny in comparison.

Large masses, such as the Earth and the Sun, attract each other with a very strong gravitational force. This is why they don't move away from one another in space.

Long ago, Aristotle believed that heavy things would fall faster but in the seventeenth century Galileo showed that all objects fall at the same speed, if you can eliminate the effect of the air particles. Objects with a large mass are pulled with a greater gravitational force than lighter ones but they also need more force to get them moving in the first place (they have greater inertia) so, in the absence of air, they all fall at the same speed.

When you drop an object on the moon, there is no air to get in the way of that falling object so all objects fall at the same rate. (You can see this in action if you watch the feather and hammer experiment by David Scott on Apollo 15, on YouTube or Brian Cox visiting the huge vacuum chamber at NASA's Space Power Facility.)

However, the shape of the objects can change the way they fall when air is present. Wider, flatter objects like the feather, will have to bump into more air particles to reach the ground than a small, compact object like the hammer. When the object bumps into air particles, the speed is reduced. A feather, in air on Earth, will fall more slowly than a hammer because of its larger surface area and the greater number of air particles it will encounter on the way down. We call this slowing force air resistance.

Galileo showed that a large ball and a small ball fall at very similar speeds because they have similar shapes. The air resistance on each is very similar because they are both compact and have relatively small surface areas. It is the surface area that makes a difference to the speed at which objects fall through air, not their mass.

Children, like Aristotle, will often believe that a heavy object will fall faster than a lighter one. As, teachers we need to let them experience objects of different shapes falling through the air in many different activities. There will inevitably be moments when children think they have proof that heavier objects fall faster than lighter ones but there will be other factors, which are impossible to eliminate in the classroom, skewing their results. If that occurs, return to the experiment on the moon with the feather and the hammer and show them that, without air, the two objects fall at the same rate.

 ## DEMO: Zeppelins

You will need:

- two sheets of A4 paper
- drawings/photographs of zeppelins
- helium balloon
- small objects to tie to the balloon, e.g. Paperlips
- large scissors.

 ## Storify the science

Read the first three chapters to the children. Spend a little time getting to know the characters and the setting. Lyra spends much of her time exploring the hidden corners of Oxford with her friends. She loves to be up high on the rooftops. Discuss the dangers of falling. She has no parents to guide her, only scholars.

Ask what the scholars would say to Lyra about falling – what might they teach her about? Draw out the topic of gravity and spend a little time exploring what the children already know.

When you reach the first mention of a zeppelin in Chapter 3 make sure that all the children know what a zeppelin looks like. Have drawings ready to help those that have not encountered one before. Ask the children to explain how they stay up.

Ask the children why the zeppelin is not falling down.

Set the challenge

We are going to think about the forces at work when something falls.

How to organise the lesson as a demonstration

Present the children with a helium balloon. You could let one or two of them feel the upward buoyant force of the balloon.

Ask – What would happen if we let go of the balloon outside?

The balloon would float away but the zeppelin does not. Discuss how the zeppelin neither rises nor falls but floats at a certain level. The bag of gas is being pushed up (no need to explain why at this stage).

Ask – How can we use gravity to make the helium balloon hang in the air so that it neither rises nor falls, just like the zeppelin?

Hang paperclips from the string to make it float at a constant height in the air. Discuss how the two forces are balanced – the force of gravity is pulling down the same amount as the buoyant force of the balloon is pushing upward. Draw a diagram of the balloon on the board with an arrow to show the force of gravity pulling down on the hanging objects and an arrow to show the buoyant force of the balloon acting upwards on the objects. Draw the arrows equal in size.

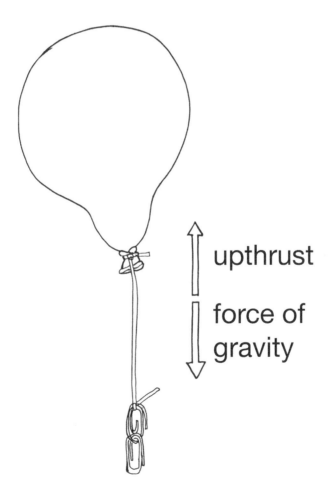

upthrust

force of gravity

Hold up a pair of scissors.

Ask – What would happen if I cut the string?

Elicit from the children that the balloon would go up and hit the ceiling.

Dramatically get out your scissors (minding eyes, of course) and make it look as if you will cut the string. Change course at the last minute. Don't cut the string. Instead, snip a large hole in the top of the balloon. Do it quickly enough to shock the children. Watch it plummet to the floor. Oh No!
The zeppelin has crashed.

Ask – What happened? Why is the balloon now on the floor?

Don't feel you have to explain why the balloon was floating before, focus instead on the fact that it fell.

Elicit from the children that the force of gravity was able to pull the object down because the balloon was no longer being forced upwards. They will probably be able to tell you now that the gas inside the balloon has now escaped so the balloon can no longer float.

Next, take the two sheets of A4 paper. Keeping them flat, safely stand on a chair (or small step ladder if that is the Health and Safety advice in your school) and hold them out in front of you in a flat position, as if they were resting on a table.

Ask – Which sheet of paper will hit the ground first?

Encourage questions and observations, e.g. The one on the right looks bigger. You must keep them at the same height. It's not fair. You mustn't throw one down as you'll 'help it win'.

Keep them guessing until you have their full attention and now scrunch up one sheet in a fairly tight ball and, without pausing for their cries of 'CHEAT!', drop them from the same height. The scrunched sheet will quickly hit the ground while the flat sheet meanders down after it. You get the best reaction if you scrunch up the paper that they had decided was the slowest.

Ask – What's the matter? Why do you think I cheated? Why did they fall differently?

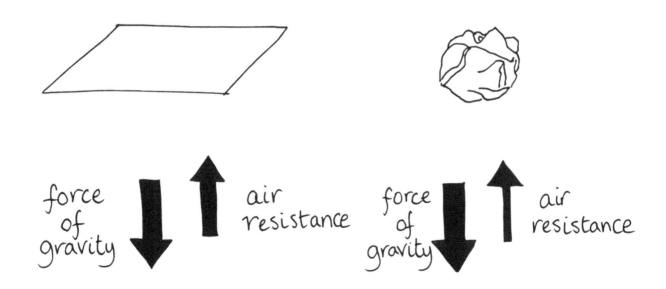

Gather their ideas and lead them to the fact that the flat sheet was bumping into air as it went down. Explain that this has a name – air resistance and that it is a force that slows things down. It is only present when objects are moving through the air.

Draw a diagram on the board of the forces working in opposite directions – the force of gravity pulling down while air resistance works in the opposite direction to the movement, i.e. up!

Ask – Which force was bigger? How do you know?

The force of gravity, when you drop the paper, was greater than the air resistance, otherwise the paper would have risen like the balloon (or floated in mid air if the forces were balanced).

Get back on the chair/stepladder and take two new sheets of paper.

Ask – What shall I try this time?

They may want you to ball it tighter. Try to demonstrate, using their ideas, that flatter shapes fall more slowly while the scrunched balls or paper folded many times falls quite quickly.

If you have plenty of scrap paper to use up, let the children try dropping their own shapes. Check health and safety regulations at your school before letting children climb on chairs.

 ## Teacher's top tips

When you burst the helium balloon, you may need to push it against a wall or hold it still as the balloon will tend to float away when prodded.

When you do a demo like this, it is good to practise first so you can keep talking and engaging your pupils while you do the demonstration.

Draw lots of diagrams with arrows to show the forces. Encourage children to show you their ideas as diagrams with arrows to show the forces. Diagrams can make invisible forces much clearer for children. Show how the forces can act in different directions and 'cancel each other out'.

 ## What next?

If you want to record your findings in a creative way then you could:

- Dress up as a scholar and prepare a lecture on gravity and air resistance to be given to Lyra as a warning about playing on the roof;

- Role-play: being a news reporter. Give a news report about a zeppelin accident where the gas bag has ruptured and the zeppelin falls from the sky. Make sure you explain the forces involved. You could then write an article about it.

- Research the use of parachutes and how they use air resistance to save people. Make parachutes that slow the fall of a small doll and explain the forces involved. (You can find more about this on p. 185 in the Alice chapter.)

Assessing children's understanding

The following statements are indicators of basic understanding:

- The gravitational force of the Earth pulls us down towards the centre of the Earth.
- Forces can act in opposite directions.
- Flat objects with a large surface area bump into lots of air particles and this slows their fall. There is a lot of air resistance.

More advanced understanding:

- When the balloon is not moving up or down in the air it is because there are forces acting upon it that are balanced.
- Air resistance is a force that acts in the opposite direction to the movement of the object. It slows the movement down.
- There is no air on the Moon so there is no air resistance.

Patterns they may be able to describe:

- The larger the surface area of a moving object, the greater the air resistance will be.

 ## INVESTIGATION: Falling objects – autogyros (spinners)

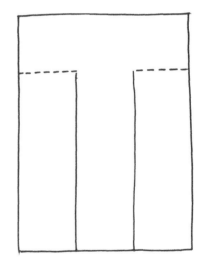

You will need:

- photocopies of the autogyro template
- squared paper
- rulers
- paperclips of various sizes.

 ## Storify the science

Remind the children of the zeppelin dropping and the paper falling and recap on the forces of gravity and air resistance.

Show the children how to cut out and fold the autogyro template and affix the paperclip at the bottom. Show them how to hold the autogyro but don't drop it. Let them find out what happens for themselves.

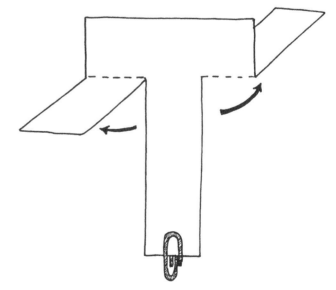

Set the challenge

First we are going to figure out how these autogyros work by making one. This will be our 'control autogyro'.

Then we are going to use what we know to investigate autogyros and make some more autogyros. We can make predictions about which one will hit the ground first and then test out our ideas by racing the new autogyros against the control autogyro.

When you make your test autogyros, think about:

*   which variable you are changing and try to keep all the others the same;
*   what you are expecting to happen – write down your predictions and comment on whether you were correct after you have your results.

When you test your autogyros, think about:

*   how you will test them fairly;
*   what you will measure;
*   how many times you need to test them to be sure you have the right answer.

Teacher's top tips

Let the children play with the control autogyro and see that it turns as it falls. Encourage them to work out how to make it twist the other way (fold the wings in the opposite direction). Let them try it out for a few minutes and practise racing one against the other.

Once they understand how it works they will find it easier to tell you which variables can be changed. Write all the possible variables on the board and encourage them to only change one thing. You'll need to guide the children to find out what makes a difference to how fast the autogyro falls by changing a variable that might affect the air resistance. If they change the size of the wings, they should try to keep everything else the same:

*   same paper
*   same size of paper
*   same paperclip.

If you provide paperclips of different sizes then they actively have to choose the right ones.

They might try:

*   large autogyro vs small (i.e. Same design reduced on photocopier);
*   large wings vs small (see diagram on facing page);
*   paper vs card;
*   holes cut in wings vs no holes.

Avoid adding paperclips as this will make it fall faster. Extra weight doesn't make things fall faster (see p. 146). But, for a host of complex reasons that we won't cover here, autogyros with

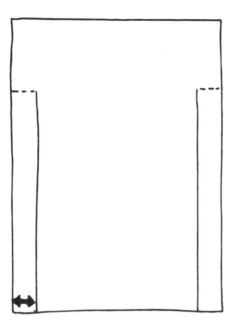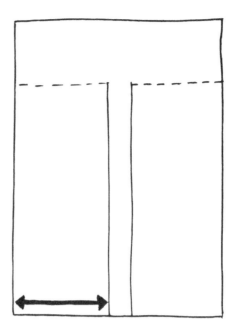

lots of paper clips do fall faster. So, show interest and explain that that does seem odd but reiterate that it isn't falling faster because it's heavier and suggest they try something from the list above that will reinforce that increasing the effective wing size will slow the fall.

It is hard to time such a short interval with hand held timers so you may just want to note which one hits the ground first.

Draw diagrams showing the air resistance is greater on the one with larger wings. Remember, that if two autogyros are made from the same size piece of paper, then the force of gravity will be the same on each one but if one is shaped so that the wings have greater surface area then the air resistance will be larger on that one.

If you want to link to maths, then use squared paper and calculate the surface area (count the squares) of the wings and time the speed of the fall and you'll have data you can plot on a line graph. You may be able to draw a straight line graph from this data and therefore use it to predict intermediate values. However, do note that they stop working at a certain size so the line on the graph won't keep going up forever.

Encourage the children to try each test enough times to be sure that they know which one hits the floor first. Make it clear to the children that the test should be repeated to make sure that the results are repeatable. They often think that repeating it makes the test fair when in reality we are checking that the result is not a fluke.

What results should I expect?

The autogyros with large wings will fall more slowly as long as the wings stay in position without flopping backwards and letting the air rush past.

Autogyros made out of floppy materials don't work because the wings flop backwards and don't stay in the right position to catch the air.

Autogyros made of card work fairly well if they are small. Large ones tend to be top heavy and don't hang in the correct position in the air.

If you make holes in the wings, they fall faster as the air rushes through the holes.

What next?

- Prepare three or four 'lantern slides' with diagrams to report what you found out in your investigation in the form of a lecture at Jordan College, for the scholars or students.
- Write a set of instructions for Lyra to make an autogyro to launch from her bedroom window. Explain how it works and draw diagrams to show the forces.
- Write a letter to Lord Asriel from Lyra where she persuades him that she is learning something useful while playing on the rooftops and dropping autogyros onto the grass below.

Assessing children's understanding

The following statements are indicators of basic understanding:

- The autogyro is pulled down by gravity.
- The wings of the autogyro are bumping into air particles and this slows it down. This is called air resistance.
- Big wings make the autogyro fall slowly.
- Small wings make the autogyro fall quickly.

More advanced understanding:

- The bigger autogyros (with wings that stay in the right position) have larger surface areas and therefore there is more air resistance acting on them. This makes them slower.
- If you increase the effective surface area of the wing, you increase the air resistance.
- If you make holes in the wings, you reduce the surface area of the wing and the autogyro will fall faster than one of the same size without holes.
- Some materials are no use because they are too floppy to withstand the force of the air pushing up on them.

Patterns they may be able to describe:

- The bigger the wings, the slower they fall (as long as the wings stay in the right position).

CANALS AND NARROW BOATS – FLOATING

Story link

The gyptians live on boats.

THE SCIENCE: Floating objects and upthrust

The children need to know that some objects float on water while others do not. A common misconception is that heavy objects sink while light objects float. However, a cruise ship is extremely heavy and yet it floats. It is the overall density of the boat in comparison to the density of the water that makes the difference – see below.

The children also need to know that the force that pushes a floating boat up in the water is called upthrust.

You might want to understand floating a little better in order to teach it. If so, you'll need to understand density.

Some materials are heavy for their size. A cube of one material can be much heavier than a cube of the exact same size of a different material. The heavier one is more dense.

All materials are made from tiny molecules packed together. If they are packed together very tightly, they will be more dense than a material that is less tightly packed. To find the exact density of a material you need to know how heavy each molecule is, how large each molecule is and how closely packed they are. In a very dense material, the molecules would be small and heavy and tightly packed together so there is a lot of stuff in a small space.

Materials float on a liquid if they are less dense than that liquid.

Air is much less dense than water so materials that contain pockets of air will tend to be less dense than water and the air pockets will give that material some buoyancy in the water. Likewise, the hull of a ship may be made from dense steel but as it is hollow, it is filled with air and the overall density of the hull is lower than the water it floats upon.

When you fill a hull with goods, the overall density of that hull increases, compared to an empty hull, especially if you fill that hull with dense materials. The ship will float lower in the water as a result. If you fill the hull with water then the overall density is more than water and the ship sinks.

Boats are designed to float level in the water so that they do not tip and take on water, causing it to sink.

Salty water contains both water and salt so it is more dense than fresh water. It is easier to float in very salty water (such as the Dead Sea) than in fresh water.

Now let's think about the forces on a floating object. The force of gravity pulls down on the floating boat and yet the boat does not sink because it has a lower overall density. The boat is pushed up by the water, of greater density, below it. We call this force upthrust. You can feel it when you push an empty water bottle, with its lid on, into water. If pushed to the bottom, it will be forced up again.

When a boat floats, the forces of gravity and upthrust are balanced. In salty water, there is greater upthrust.

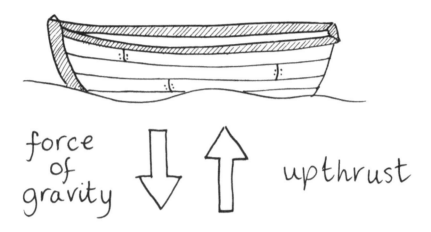

ACTIVITY: Making boats that are stable

You will need:

- foil take-away container trays (available at the cash and carry – the long and thin ones look most like narrow boats)
- marbles
- 100 g masses or whatever is available
- stones
- modelling clay
- large water tanks/washing up bowls/watertight plastic boxes
- card
- scissors
- soft foams or plastics that are easily cut to shape.

Storify the science

Put the tank of water where all can see it.

Read Chapter 6 and talk about the gyptians. They live on narrow boats in a large community and Lyra has encountered them before.

Place one tin foil tray into the water to represent the gyptian boat and add a dense object (such as a 100 g mass) into the centre to represent the cargo or people. Look at the way it floats in the water. Introduce the idea that, as it is not sinking, something must be holding it up.

Discuss going swimming – you can feel the water holding you up.

Near the beginning of Chapter 2, Lyra convinces her friends to search out the bung on one of the narrow boats as she believes that pulling out the bung would cause the boat to sink. Revisit this part of the text. Discuss what would happen if there was indeed a bung and the bung was pulled out. Now place another tin foil tray into the water that has a small hole punched in the base such as a hole for a bung. Place the same dense object into this boat and observe what happens. Discuss how it only sinks to the bottom when it is full of water.

Now add marbles to the tin tray that has no hole. Deliberately add them in such a way that the marbles roll to one end and sink the boat. You can either drop them into one end or tip it up with waves. Notice that before it sinks, only one end of the boat is in contact with the water – not the entire base of the boat.

 ## Set the challenge

You must design a boat for the gyptians to carry their family and goods in a way that will not cause the boat to sink. Your boat must carry a cargo of marbles (however many sank the boat before) and the marbles will be dropped into the boat and there will be waves to check the stability of your design on the sea. You will all start with a foil tray. You can change the shape of the tray and add things to it to create your design.

When you make your boat think about:

- the shape of the hull;
- how you will stabilise the cargo so it won't all end up at one end if it encounters a big wave.

Take care not to make holes in the foil or you will need a bung!

 ## Teacher's top tips

This activity is designed to let them feel the upthrust under the boat and to be aware that a large flat hull such as a narrow boat provides a large surface area on which upthrust can act, so give them time to play and feel the forces.

Keep talking about gravity pulling down and upthrust pushing up.

When you add the marbles to test the boats, make sure you drop the marbles all over the boat rather than all at one end. Don't deliberately sink them but do then tip the boat a little to make sure the marbles don't move. Hopefully, the children will find ways to make compartments within the boats to stop the marbles moving.

Draw diagrams with arrows to show the force of gravity pulling the boat down and the upthrust of the water acting in the opposite direction.

The children may choose to make their boat more streamlined with a pointed bow at the front. You can choose to discuss this and relate it to speed if you choose at this point. You will find the science you need on p. 170 when we look at streamlining with the broomstick investigation, later in this chapter.

Have spare foil trays ready as they can develop cracks if bent too much.

Give the children time to see other designs and spend some time evaluating their own design. Encourage them to think about what worked well and what they would improve next time.

What results should I expect?

The children should manage to design a boat with compartments so the cargo cannot end up all in one end. As long as the loaded boat can be tipped up to about 45 degrees without the marbles all running to one end, the boat design can be considered successful.

Little extras

The density of saltwater is greater than fresh water so the gyptians' boats would float better on the saltwater. You could do this little demo to get the children thinking about the difference between saltwater and fresh:

Before the lesson, prepare a tall clear jug of fresh water and one of very salty water – dissolve as much as you can in the water without leaving visible grains at the bottom. Gently lower an egg into each jug. The egg in saltwater should float higher in the water. Discuss why this might be so. They will probably tell you the eggs are different so at this point, swap the eggs over. Once they begin to suspect there is something in the water you can elicit the real reason from them. Link back to the gyptians and their boats floating differently in saltwater and fresh. Talk about the forces – there is greater upthrust in the saltwater.

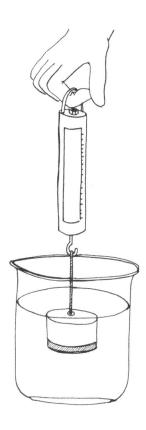

If you want to go further, you can measure the different amounts of upthrust by lowering hanging masses into the jugs, suspended from a newton metre. Begin by measuring the weight of the hanging masses in air, then lower the hanging masses into the different jugs until the masses are under water but not touching the bottom. The newton metre will show that the hanging masses appear to weigh less in the water than they do in air as the upthrust of the water will support them. They will appear to weigh even less in the saltwater than the fresh water as their mass is supported more by the greater upthrust of the saltwater.

What next?

If you want to record your findings in a creative way then you could:

*   Role-play a conversation between Lyra and Tony Costa in which Lyra asks lots of questions about why the boat floats and Tony Costa explains the forces. Write this down as a playscript. You could even film it.

*   Write a mini book about narrow boats and their design. Draw the boat you designed and annotate it to show how you made it stable and the forces involved in making it float.

*   Write instructions for making a stable narrow boat, explaining why each part is built that way.

*   Use a digital storytelling app (there are many on the internet that can be downloaded onto iPads and tablets) to make a presentation where the children's drawings become the video element and their voices are recorded over the top, explaining the design of the narrow boat and the forces involved in making it float.

Assessing children's understanding

The following statements are indicators of basic understanding:

*   A boat will float on water because the water is pushing up on it – this upward pushing force is called upthrust.

*   Objects float more easily in saltwater.

More advanced understanding:

*   When an object sinks through the water, there is not enough upthrust to overcome the downward pull of the force of gravity.

*   When an object floats in water, it has a lower overall density than the water.

*   Saltwater contains both salt and water so it is more dense than fresh water.

*   There is more upthrust in saltwater because it is more dense.

Patterns they may be able to describe:

*   When you increased the density of the water by adding salt to it the upthrust increases. Therefore, the saltier the water, the greater the upthrust. N.B. There is a limit to how much salt can be dissolved in water therefore this pattern will only continue until that limit is reached.

SLEDGES – SLIDING

Story link
Lyra travels by sledge.

THE SCIENCE: Friction

When a sledge slides over snow, it glides easily. However, when you drag the same sledge over gravel, the sledge will be much harder to pull along and, if pushed and left to glide on gravel, the sledge will quickly grind to a halt. Friction is the force that slows the sledge down. Whenever two surfaces are in contact with each other, there will be a degree of friction. There is very little friction between the sledge runners and the snow so it glides easily. There is a lot of friction between the runners and gravel.

Surfaces may not slide easily over one another for several reasons:

- There may be rough edges that catch on each other so that they cannot run smoothly over one another without knocking those bumps off or moving a little apart to hop over the top.

- Surfaces may stick/adhere to each other, there may even be chemical bonds between the two surfaces that must be broken in order for the surfaces to slide over one another, e.g. glass on glass.

- One surface may press into the other, because it is heavy, denting it so that it ploughs a kind of groove in the other and this can make it harder to move.

What do the children need to know?

- Friction is a force that slows you down. It works in the opposite direction to movement.

- Some surfaces grip one another well. More force is required to slide something over a grippy surface because there is a lot of friction acting in the opposite direction to the movement, slowing the movement down.

- Friction can be useful; we need our shoes to grip the floor so that they don't slip back-~wards as we push off to go forwards; chairs that are too shiny and slippery are not easy to sit on.

INVESTIGATION: Sledges and reducing the friction

You will need:

- small blocks of wood with a hook at one end or take-away containers with string attached
- 100 g masses
- ramps

- ramp stands or piles of books to elevate one end of the ramp
- strips of different materials to lay over the ramps
- newton metres (calibrated from 0–10 N).

You can buy ready-made ramps covered in different materials from educational suppliers with stands and also ready-made wooden sledges with hooks.

 Storify the science

Read Chapter 11. It leads up to the journey north by sledge. Linger on the part where Lyra's sledge sets off through the town and later over the fresh snow, at the end of the chapter. Ask the children why the motion of the sledge becomes swift and smooth once they reach the fresh snow. Children may be able to tell you from experience that sledges are really hard to pull over concrete or gravel but easy over compacted snow.

If they have no experience of sledges, get them talking about walking in shoes vs socks on a slippery floor and whether it is easier when running to skid on a slippery floor in shoes, or in socks. They may also talk about making skids in ice. Elicit from them that some surfaces are grippy while others are slippy.

Introduce the idea that when two surfaces grip together, this is called friction and it is friction that slowed Lyra's sledge down on the gravel and made it hard work for the dogs.

 Set the challenge

You are going to investigate which surfaces create the most friction.

First, look at all the different surfaces, feel them and predict which one you think will create the most friction, such as the gravel, and the least friction, such as the snow.

You will need to set up a ramp on a slope. You are going to drag the sledge uphill using the newton metre. When the sledge starts to move at a slow but steady speed, read the newton metre to see how much force is required to move the sledge.

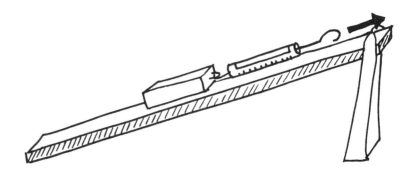

Then change the surface of the ramp and repeat the experiment.

Think about:

*   how you will make the test fair;
*   how you will record your results;
*   whether your results will be the same as the rest of the class.

What do your results show? Can you explain your results?

Teacher's top tips

The reason I suggest using a ramp, rather than a level surface, is to make it harder to move the sledge. A smooth bottomed sledge on a smooth ramp will move so easily that it may not register any force on the newton metre. If you find that the sledges still move too easily and the force is hard to measure, place a 100 g mass on the sledge to weight it down and make it harder to move. As long as the same mass is used for the whole experiment, it will be fair.

It doesn't matter exactly how high the ramp is, as long as it stays the same throughout the experiment. This will mean that different groups get different readings on the newton metres as the higher the ramp the greater the force required to move it. They should all find that certain very rough or sticky/grippy surfaces give the highest results.

Good materials to try are:

*   sandpaper
*   rubber
*   carpet
*   smooth plastic
*   corrugated cardboard
*   bubble wrap
*   doormat
*   smooth wood
*   the rubber gripper you put under carpets to stop them moving.

Let the children practise gently pulling the sledge with the newton metre until the sledge just starts moving steadily. It's a hard skill. If they work in pairs or threes, one child can pull while the other reads.

You may find you have a range of different newton metres in your school rather than a matching set. It is worth investing in a set of 10 newton metres, all calibrated from 0–10 N so you can do class investigations such as this.

You may find you have a set of sledges at your school with different surfaces

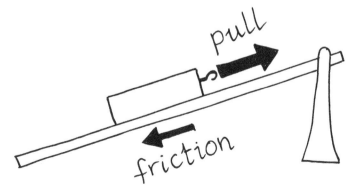

stuck to the bottom of each sledge. In this case, use a plain ramp and change the sledge each time.

You can use this opportunity to gather data to teach data handling and record as bar charts etc.

Draw lots of diagrams using arrows to show that the force of friction acts in the opposite direction to movement and slows moving objects down.

What results should I expect?

Rubber, rough matting and sandpaper tend to give the highest results. The rubber sticks to the other surface, giving it more grip, whilst the sandpaper and rough matting may get their rough surfaces caught on each other. Therefore, there will be more force required to drag a sledge over these surfaces than on a smooth surface as there is more friction at work.

What next?

If you want to record your findings in a creative way then you could:

- Draw a graph to show your results and write a lab report for a sledge manufacturer in Trollesund, Lapland, explaining the forces at play and which surface created the least friction.
- Design a sledge that could travel over any surface. You could give it imaginary gadgets that could reduce the friction, e.g. a snow sprayer at the front.
- Write an owner's manual explaining the workings of the sledge in which Lyra travels.
- Role-play: Pan pulling Lyra on a sledge. Talk to each other about how Pan, as a small ermine, can pull Lyra on the snow.

Assessing children's understanding

The following statements are indicators of basic understanding:

- It is harder to pull a sledge on a sticky or rough surface.
- The force that stops the sledge moving is friction.
- There is more friction on the sticky or rough surfaces.

More advanced understanding:

- Some surfaces stick together, which stops the sledge moving, increasing the friction. Other surfaces are rough so their rough edges catch on each other and this stops the sledge moving by increasing the friction.

Patterns they may be able to describe:

- Smoother surfaces are more slippery and have less friction than rough surfaces. However, some smooth surfaces are sticky or grippy so this pattern will not apply.

BEAR FEET – GRIPPING

Story link

The polar bear can run on the snow and ice.

THE SCIENCE: Friction

Polar bears are well adapted to life in the frozen north. Their paws are larger than those of most bears, acting like snow shoes by spreading the weight of their large bodies and preventing the bear from sinking into the snow. They also have webbing between the toes of their front paws to further increase the surface area of their feet, thus spreading their weight. Their claws do not retract which is useful for gripping the ice. Underneath, they have bumps on the skin of their pads and long stiff hairs between their toes that all help to increase the friction their feet have on the slippery snow so they have enough grip to push off and move forwards.

INVESTIGATION: Bear feet and increasing the friction

You will need:

- shoes of all kinds – trainers, ballet shoes, school shoes, snow boots, small wellies etc. and all the children's own school shoes
- tables with smooth tops

- newton metres
- scales
- 100 g and 50 g masses
- string.

Storify the science

Read the first few pages of Chapter 12, up to the part where Lyra is riding on Iorek's back. Discuss how it would feel to ride a polar bear.

Show the children photos or videos of polar bears running over snow and ice. Look closely at their physical features that help them to travel so confidently on this slippery surface.

Ask the children what the underside of Iorek's feet might be like. Explain about the bumps and hairs that give grip.

Ask questions about the kind of shoes they would need in order to run on ice.

Set the challenge

You are going to test some shoes to ascertain which type of sole is most grippy on a slippery table top. Look closely at all the shoes and feel them. Some of them look grippy and others do not. Check to see whether they are all similar in mass. If they are not, you may need to put 100 g masses inside the lighter ones so that the mass of the shoes is roughly the same. We only want to test the type of sole not the mass.

When you choose your shoes, think about:

*   whether the soles are similar in size and whether this will make a difference;
*   whether you have chosen a range of different soles to test;
*   how to attach the hook of the newton metre to make it pull the shoe along evenly.

Predict which sole you think will have the most grip on a slippery surface and be best for running on ice.

Once you have selected some different shoes to test (that are similar in mass) you can use the newton metre, like last lesson, to see how much force is required to pull it steadily across the table. Try to read the newton metre when the shoe is being dragged slowly across the table. Record your results to prove whether your prediction was correct.

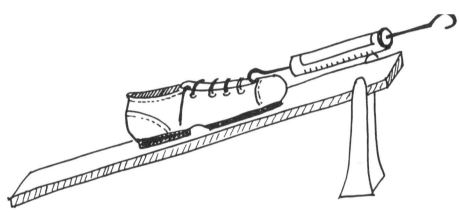

 ## Teacher's top tips

Supply a range of shoes including those that are impractical to test. If you limit the shoes they can choose from, you stop them from being able to think about it and make wise choices. Let the children work out that high heels are not designed for snow!

Likewise, supply the scales but let them work out how to make sure all the shoes have the same mass. If they choose to just compare the feel of them then that is something you can talk about at the end.

Some shoes have no obvious place to hook in the newton metre so you may need to help the children to tie string in such a way that it can be pulled horizontally across the desk by the loop of string.

Draw diagrams of the children pulling the different shoes across the table top and mark arrows for the pull force and arrows in the opposite direction to show friction. Diagrams can really help children to visualise the forces (see previous section p. 164).

What results should I expect?

Shoes are many and varied so it is hard to guess which will create the most friction. It might be flat rubber soles with no indentations that stick best to the table top or the rubber wellies with the great big indentations. It certainly won't be smooth leather soled shoes or ballet slippers.

When you talk about the experiment at the end, discuss what each shoe is designed for and whether it is fit for purpose as well as which would be best for running on ice. Ballet shoes are designed to grip the floor and yet still slide enough to allow the wearer to turn on the spot. Wellingtons are designed to keep the water out. They're not designed to stay on when running.

Use your results from the experiment and think about the practicality of the shoes for walking on snow to make your choice. Snow boots are likely to come out on top!

 # What next?

If you want to record your findings in a creative way then you could:

- Design a shoe for the frozen north, for Lyra to wear on her journey. Be very clear about the design of the sole but also consider the materials you might use to make sure Lyra's feet are warm, dry and comfortable.
- Create an advert for the shoes you have designed.
- Role-play a scene where Lyra is persuading John Faa that it is Iorek who is best suited to running on this terrain due to his adaptations for running in the snow. Explain the forces at work and how Iorek's feet are designed to increase the friction.
- Write Lyra's diary entry for the day she rode on Iorek's back and, in it, record her conversation with John Faa explaining why Iorek is best suited for the terrain.

 # Assessing children's understanding

The following statements are indicators of basic understanding:

- The rubber soles were more grippy.
- The smoother soles were easier to pull.
- There is more friction on the rubber soles with bumps.
- Rubber soles with bumps would be best on ice.

More advanced understanding:

- Some surfaces stick together, increasing the friction so even flat rubber soles can be grippy. Other soles have indentations and bumps so their edges catch on the surface below and this stops the sole from slipping by providing lots of friction.
- You can't dig spikes into the table like you could into the snow so spiky shoes, such as polar bear claws, might be even better.

BROOMSTICKS – STREAMLINING

Story link
The witches arrive on broomsticks.

THE SCIENCE: Air resistance

Air resistance comes into play whenever something is moving through air. In the first activity, we looked at air resistance on falling objects but air resistance slows moving objects that are moving horizontally through air too. Cars, trucks, trains, runners, even the top part of boats: all of these are moving through air and will bump into air particles so air resistance will slow them down. If the front of the object has a large blunt shape, it will encounter more air particles than a narrow pointed shape. This is why the fronts of vehicles made for speed are usually chisel or arrow shaped. These shapes 'cut through the air', the air particles moving past them rather than becoming trapped in front.

N.B. An object will encounter a similar resistance when it moves through water as the object bumps into water particles. More streamlined shapes will encounter less resistance from the water as they travel forwards. This is water resistance not upthrust and the boat must be moving through the water to encounter water resistance, whereas upthrust will be present all the time that the boat is floating.

INVESTIGATION: Air resistance and streamlining – shaped for speed

You will need:

- bendy straws
- larger straws of a greater diameter so that the bendy straw will fit easily inside them
- scissors
- protractors
- tape
- paper, card, straw, wool and other materials to add to the broomstick.

Storify the science

Read the rest of chapter from the part where Lyra sets out on Iorek's back and sees the witches in the sky. Ask the children to imagine riding a broomstick and think about how difficult it would be to steer and how windy it would be up there.

Encourage the children to think about the air they would feel bumping into their faces. Remind them of the autogyros they made earlier and the force of air resistance.

If you want to help the children feel the air resistance, you can choose two skilful runners (who are good sports) and ask them to put appropriate footwear on, then tell them they are going to have a race across the playground. Tape a large piece of card (which sticks out both sides and above the head) to the back of one child, like a tortoise shell, using masking tape or give them an umbrella to hold out behind them, taking care to keep spiky bits away from faces.

The class may decide that this is unfair and begin to explain that the child with the umbrella will be at a disadvantage. If not, get on with the race, repeating a few times and show that the umbrella or card will slow them down. Ask the children to explain why this happens and elicit the fact that when an object moves through air in any direction it will encounter air resistance. Those witches must have felt the air resistance on their faces as they flew.

 ## Set the challenge

You are going to investigate the force of air resistance on the witches.

Take one of each kind of straw. Post the bendy straw inside the larger straw. Check it slides in and out easily. Now take the larger straw and bend it about 3 cm from the end and tape it firmly in place so that the larger straw is now sealed at one end. This is your 'control broomstick'. Take a strip of paper and slice into it to create a fringe and then tape this fringe around the open end of your control broomstick to make a fluffy brush that will encounter some air resistance. Now you are ready to launch.

The bendy straw is your 'launcher'. Put your control broomstick on the launcher and blow hard to launch the broomstick into an empty space in the room. Make sure everyone gets out of the way! Does it fly?

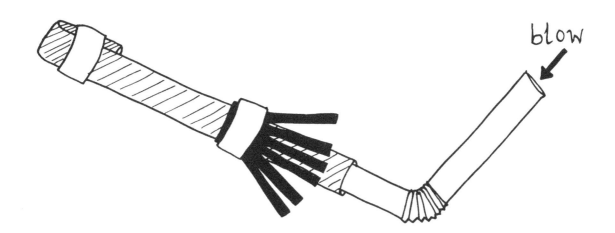
blow

You are going to make another broomstick. This will be your 'test broomstick'.

When you make your test broomstick, think about:

- the length of your broomstick;
- what you will use to make the brush and what shape the brush should be;
- how you will measure how far it flies;
- how you can be sure that your results are reliable;
- how you will reduce the air resistance on the brush.

When you launch your broomstick, think about:

- how you can make each launch as similar as possible.

Watch carefully to see how each broomstick flies. You can keep making improvements or making new test broomsticks until you are sure that your test broomstick flies as far as possible. Witches never ride bare sticks without a brush so you must add something to your test broomstick but make sure it helps your broomstick to fly well.

Teacher's top tips

Variables that may affect the flight of the broomstick include:

- shape of the brush;
- the material (mass) of the brush;
- amount of puff used to launch the broomstick;
- the length of the broomstick;
- the angle at which it is launched.

Encourage the children to try to only change one variable – the shape of the brush or the material – as this will affect the amount of air resistance. Try to keep the rest the same each time it is tested.

Encourage the children to repeat the experiment to make sure that they know their result is what usually happens and not a fluke. Children often think that we repeat experiments in order to make the test fair when in fact the process of repeating the experiment is all about checking the data for reliability.

Some children will realise that this broomstick flies like a dart or rocket and add fins that can make it fly really well. Let them try any additions to the broom. Some children will want to add straw or wool to make their broom look genuine, so provide these, even though they may weigh the broomstick down and prevent it from flying well.

Children love a competition. Let them fly their best test broomstick from a starting line at the end of a long space such as a corridor, leave them in place where they land and see which designs make it a long way. Look carefully at the designs afterwards and discuss why they went further – it may be simply the lung capacity of the launcher!

Remember that once the broomstick leaves the launcher, the push of the launcher's breath no longer affects it. In mid flight, the only forces acting on it are the force of gravity and air resistance, which act to slow its ascent and eventually bring it back down and slow it to a standstill.

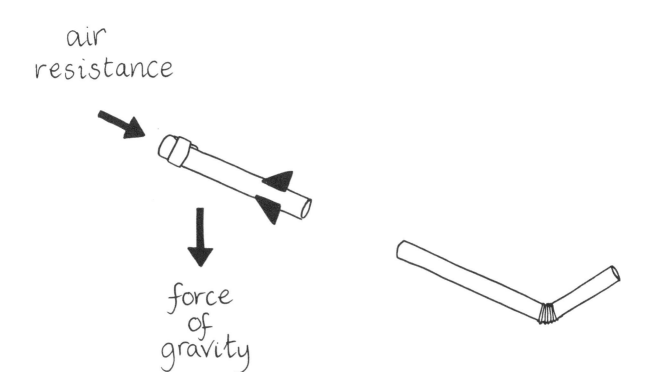

Little extras

You can extend this topic into maths and use it to teach angles. Simply tape the bendy straw to the protractor so that the mouthpiece is fixed and the launching end of the straw can be moved to a particular angle. Launching the broomstick at a particular angle can also change the distance it will fly. This should be kept at the same angle while all other factors are tested to make those tests fair. However, you could decide to test the effect of the angle of launch and keep all other factors the same whilst you change the angle.

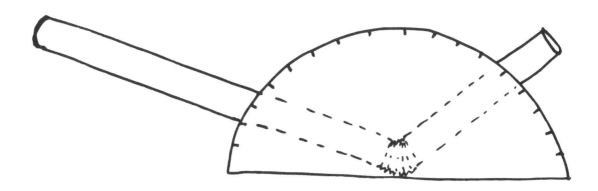

What results should I expect?

The more streamlined broomsticks encounter less air resistance and should fly further. In addition, fin-like additions may even keep the broomstick travelling straight so it flies further.

If you do the little extra activity you will find that launching the broomsticks at angles near zero degrees (i.e. horizontal) and launching at angles close to 90 degrees (i.e. vertical) won't be very successful. Broomsticks launched at about 45 degrees will fly better but the exact angle will depend on your broomstick and the child launching it.

N.B. Very long broomsticks can get stuck on the launcher.

 ## What next?

If you want to record your findings in a creative way then you could:

- Look at the witches in *The Golden Compass* film compared to the book. In the film, the witches have no broomsticks. In the book, the witches fly on any branch of 'cloud-pine'. Also, research other stories involving broomsticks, such as Harry Potter, and look for the most streamlined designs. Explain which is most streamlined and why.

- Write to Serafina Pekkala and persuade her to purchase a streamlined broom, rather than a branch of cloud-pine, explaining how this will help her, with references to the forces involved.

- Take slow-mo videos of your broomsticks in flight and write a commentary to go over the video images explaining what is happening as the broomstick is pushed up into the air by the force of the air blown through the launcher, as it flies upwards and slows due to air resistance, and as the force of gravity eventually tips it back down and it comes to a halt on the ground. You could even splice in diagrams at various points to show the forces. Then use all these parts to make a short movie about your broomstick in an app such as iMovie.

 ## Assessing children's understanding

The following statements are indicators of basic understanding:

- The broomstick with a big fluffy brush did not fly very far.
- The broomstick with a small streamlined brush flew better.
- The big fluffy brush bumped into more air.

More advanced understanding:

- The bigger, fluffier brushes encounter more air resistance so they are slower.

Patterns they may be able to describe:

- The more streamlined the broomstick, the less air resistance it encounters and the further it flies.

HOT AIR BALLOONS – UPTHRUST IN AIR

Story link
Lee Scoresby takes Lyra in his balloon.

THE SCIENCE: Density and upthrust

(See p. 155 canal boats)

Boats float because their overall density is less than that of water. Hot air balloons rise because the air inside them is less dense than the air surrounding them. How can air be less dense than air? Air spreads out more when it is heated so hot air is less dense than cold air. In fact, all gases spread out when they are heated.

Hot air balloons will be pushed upwards by the cold air around them. We call this force upthrust, just as a boat is pushed up by the upthrust of the water.

DEMO 1 AND 2: Hot gases rising

For demo 1 You will need:

- a safe indoor space in which to work with plenty of room in all directions
- foil
- flat surface
- matches
- a posh herbal tea-bag that can be unclipped and emptied to leave a cylinder of tea-bag mesh. This won't work with normal flat square or circular tea-bags. You can also use the wrapper of an amaretti biscuit, flattened out and then rolled into a cylinder. You can also find purpose-made paper called 'wish paper' or 'prayer paper' on the internet which works well but is pricey.

For demo 2 You will need:

- foil helium balloon (half or three-quarters filled with helium)
- hairdryer (check it has been safety tested).

Storify the science

Read Chapter 17 up to the point where the hot air balloon takes off and Lyra is pressed against the basket floor. Stop and give the children a chance to imagine a hot air balloon rising at speed. Discuss experiences of seeing, or even going in, hot air balloons.

What might it feel like to rise so steeply. Discuss how the author describes what the acceleration did to Lyra.

air resistance

force
of
gravity

upthrust

Ask the children what forces they think are involved.

Elicit from them that the force of gravity must be pulling the balloon down and yet it is travelling up.

Ask for suggestions as to the force that is pushing them up. The children may tell you this is air resistance but point out that as the hot air balloon is travelling upwards, it will be bumping into air above the balloon so air resistance will be slowing its travel upwards not helping it go upwards. It is upthrust.

Discuss floating in water. A boat sits on the top of the water, neither going up nor down. The hot air balloon will eventually reach the point where it neither goes up nor down. Develop an understanding that at this point the forces of gravity and upthrust will be equal and balanced.

Draw the forces as arrows on a diagram. The hot air balloon is not moving upwards now so air resistance is no longer encountered.

Tell the children they are going to investigate the force of upthrust in air. They will need to watch carefully and think about what is happening.

Hot gases rising (demo 1)

Practise this before you begin! There are lots of videos of this on YouTube.

Position the children well back from your table and ask the children to watch. You don't need to say anything else.

Cut open the tea-bag or roll up the biscuit wrapper so that you have a cylinder of tea-bag or amaretti biscuit wrapper ready. Stand the cylinder on a flat surface that has been covered in foil.

Light the match and light the top end of the cylinder in a few spots to get it burning down evenly and stand well back.

The last inch or so of ash to burn should rise up majestically into the air, float for a while and drop slowly back down again.

Ask – What happened?

Repeat the process so the children can watch again.

Ask – Why is it going up? Why only the little bit at the end? What is making it go up? The children may say that it is the heat that is making the ash go up. Follow the train of this thought.

Ask – What is the heat doing? Recap on the fact that heat will give the air molecules more energy. When molecules of gas have more energy, they spread out and become less dense so they can float on cold air.

Ask – Which forces are at work here? Elicit that gravity is pulling the ash down and upthrust is pushing the ash up. As it accelerates upwards, the effect of the upthrust is larger than the force of gravity. Draw these two forces on a diagram of the ash rising in the same way as the hot air balloon diagram above.

Now go on to the next demo.

 ## Teacher's top tips

Some tea-bags work better than others so try a few brands to find the best.

Practise this before you try it at school as the flames can seem alarming as it burns down.

Make sure there are no draughts that will topple the tea-bag over.

Make sure your tea-bag stands on the foil.

Check the health and safety rules at your school to check you are allowed to use matches in the classroom without setting off fire alarms etc.

Make sure all children stay well back.

Helium balloon rising (demo 2)

First, prepare your foil helium balloon. This needs to be done before the lesson – you may be able to get the balloon shop to do this for you. The balloon needs to hover in mid air without going up or down. For this to happen, you will need to only half or three-quarter fill the balloon. You can leave the string on if you have very high ceilings or remove it. Helium is an inert gas and won't set alight but you will want to make sure that it won't bump into anything sharp or hot when it rises.

Show the children the balloon.

Ask – Why is it not rising? Gather suggestions. They may be able to tell you that the force of gravity and the force of upthrust are balanced at this point, like competitors of equal strength pulling on a rope in a tug of war when the rope doesn't move.

Hold the balloon in one hand and use the hairdryer to warm it. It should visibly expand and look full and tight. When you let go it will rise up.

Ask – What is happening?

The balloon should begin to fall as the helium cools and you can repeat the demo.

Keep discussing what is happening. Elicit from the children that the heat made the helium gas spread out, making the balloon expand. Link this to density. When the gas spreads out, the balloon becomes less dense because the same mass of gas is now taking up more space. When it is less dense than air, it will rise.

Ask – What forces are at work? Draw the force of upthrust pushing up and the force of gravity pulling down. When the balloon is warm and the gas inside is less dense, then the force of upthrust is greater than the force of gravity.

Relate this to the hot air balloon. When the air in the balloon is heated, the air particles spread out and become less dense than the air around the balloon and upthrust pushes the hot air balloon up.

N.B. The children may know that helium is less dense than air and may wonder why the helium balloon doesn't rise when it is half full. You can explain that helium itself is less dense than air but when considering the balloon we have to consider the foil too. The overall density of a foil balloon full of helium is less than the density of air. But the overall density of a half-filled balloon might be equal to the density of air and will, therefore, hover. If it sinks, then the overall density must be greater than that of air.

 ## Teacher's top tips

Always practise at home before you do this in front of the children.

Buy a foil balloon not a rubber one. This demo won't work with a rubber balloon.

Helium balloons will get very tight in a hot car and very saggy in a cold room as the gas inside expands in heat and contracts in the cold. When you go to buy your balloon, be aware that it may hover beautifully in mid air in the warm shop and then sink when you take it home to a chilly house. If you use the string as ballast, you can always cut some string off to help it float if it is cooler at school.

Buy your balloon the night before to get the best results.

 ## What next?

If you want to record your findings in a creative way then you could:

- Role-play a conversation between Lyra and Lee Scoresby where Lyra is trying to understand how the hot air balloon rises and Lee is explaining the forces involved.
- Write an owner's manual for Lee Scoresby giving instructions and tips on how to inflate a hot air balloon and how to get the balloon to lift into the air.
- Write an entry in Lee Scoresby's log/journal where he explains that he had to carry Iorek in his balloon and documents the extra upthrust he had to generate in order to overcome the added weight of the bear. Include diagrams to show the forces.

 ## Assessing children's understanding

The following statements are indicators of basic understanding:

- The ash went upwards because it had hot air inside.
- The balloon went up because the gas inside spread out.
- The upwards force is called upthrust.

More advanced understanding:

- The ash/balloon started to go up because the upthrust was greater than the force of gravity.
- The ash rose because its overall density (including the hot air inside it) was less than that of the air around it.
- Helium is less dense than air.
- The full helium balloon floats in air because its overall density is less than that of air.
- When you warm a gas it spreads out and becomes less dense.

Patterns they may be able to describe:

- The warmer the helium in the balloon, the less dense it became.

ZEPPELINS AND CREATING THRUST

Story link

Mrs Coulter chases Lyra in her zeppelin.

THE SCIENCE: Thrust – a push force

Thrust is essentially a push force. For children at primary school, that is enough explanation. You can create thrust with jet engines or a propeller. The children will be familiar with the experience of a propeller or jet pushing a vehicle forwards like an aeroplane or upwards like a helicopter or a rocket.

To understand how a propeller propels an aircraft forward by pushing air out backwards you need to understand a little about Newton's third law of motion. This states that for every action there is an equal and opposite reaction, This can be demonstrated by a child standing on a skate board next to a wall. If they apply a force to the wall, i.e. push it, they will move in the opposite direction. The wall 'pushes' back with exactly the same force as the child has pushed.

A propeller on an aeroplane works by pushing air backwards. The air subsequently pushes back on the aeroplane with the same force thus propelling the aeroplane forward.

ACTIVITY: Designing propellers

You will need:

- batteries (enough to power all the motors – two AA batteries are usually enough for one motor)
- wires with crocodile clips (two per motor)
- electric motors (one per pair of children)
- card cut into small squares (5 cm x 5 cm)
- other material, e.g. craft foam and paper cut into small squares (5 cm by 5 cm)
- scissors
- thick elastic bands cut into small sections (approximately 6mm long)
- scrap paper cut into tiny pieces
- large helium filled balloon
- fans or hairdryers to observe
- drawing pins.

 ## Storify the science

Build the tension as you read Chapters 21 and 22. Create the sense of urgency that Roger has been taken. Keep reading until you reach the part where Lyra hears the zeppelin approaching and then stop. Discuss the zeppelin. Discuss what it might have looked like and how loud the engines might be.

Discuss how fast it could move and how it would be buffeted by the winds.

Talk about how much force would be required to move a zeppelin – would it be easy? Which forces might slow it down. If you can, watch YouTube clips of Guy Martin and his attempt to cross the channel on an airship. The challenges of trying to steer an enormous balloon in the wind, and keeping it at a good height, are clear to see.

 ## Set the challenge

We are going to make a helium balloon zeppelin model move.

Your challenge is to make a propeller that creates enough thrust to move the zeppelin.

First look closely at the fans or hairdryers to see the shape of the propeller/fan blades.

Next you will need to make a complete circuit with the batteries, the wires and the motor to make sure all your components work.

Now you need to design a propeller. Use the card to cut out a shape. Use a drawing pin to make a tiny hole for the shaft of the motor. Also make a tiny hole, with the pin, in a piece of elastic band. Push the card onto the shaft, through the hole and secure it by putting the elastic band piece on after it.

Now turn the motor on. Does it create a draught? Can you move the scrap paper pieces with the force of the draught? Think about ways to improve your propeller design. Keep trying until you find a really effective shape for your propeller.

You will need to think about:

- the material you chose for your propeller;
- the number of blades;
- the angle of your blades;
- the size of your blades;
- the shape of your blades.

The most effective propellers will blow tiny scrap paper pieces across the table. Can yours?

Teacher's top tips

The best materials are those that will hold their shape, such as card but supply materials that don't work so well so that the children have to make that choice.

If you cut the card into a circle and snip in from the edge to the centre, you can divide the card into as many blades as you like with minimal cutting. Now take each blade and twist it in the same direction so that the card is no longer flat but resembles a fan. Demonstrate this for children who are struggling.

Try this yourself before the lesson, so you know what will work and can guide the children.

You may need to increase the power to the motor by adding batteries to get enough thrust to move the zeppelin. School motors tend to be 6V so they can be powered by up to four 1.5v AA batteries. However, this will increase the weight on the balloon so you may have to try this in advance to get the balloon to hover.

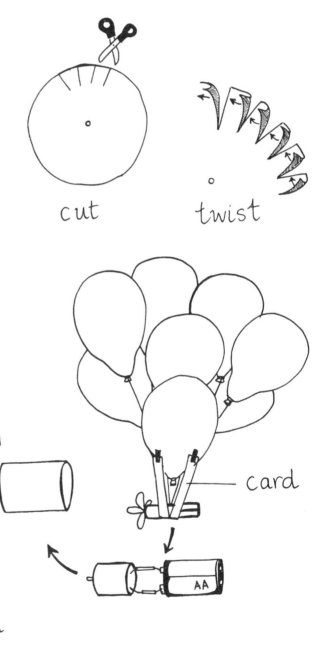

I have found that a standard school motor in a clip, with two AA batteries in a battery clip will require about eight helium balloons to support the weight. Even the largest foil balloons are too small to provide sufficient upthrust to hold up the 100 g that the motor and battery weigh. However, bundling eight to ten regular-sized, helium-filled latex balloons together was enough and flew well, as long as the motor was properly fixed as shown on the previous page.

You may want to include a switch in your design but this will add extra weight.

 # Finale

When the children have had enough time to design a working propeller, test each one to find the most effective at moving scrap paper pieces across the table. Then, take the winner and attach it to the helium balloon as shown above.

You will need to adjust the ballast (and maybe even buy a spare balloon) to make sure the zeppelin stays at a constant height in the air. Once you are happy that the zeppelin is ready to fly, launch her with due pomp and ceremony and watch her cruise across the classroom.

 # What next?

If you want to record your findings in a creative way then you could:

- Photograph or film your zeppelin launch and write a news report, including an interview with the engineer who can explain how the propeller was designed.
- Draw an annotated diagram as if you were the engineer. Label the parts and the forces involved in getting the zeppelin to fly. It could be an exploded diagram where the propeller is larger to show the detail of the design.
- Role-play a factual TV programme on propeller design. Talk about and demonstrate propellers that were successful and those that weren't.

 # Assessing children's understanding

The following statements are indicators of basic understanding:

- The propellers push the zeppelin along.
- The blades of a propeller need to be the right shape to make the air move.

More advanced understanding:

- The propeller moves the air and this creates thrust that pushes the zeppelin forward.

Patterns they may be able to describe:

- The faster the motor, the greater the thrust.

7 *Alice's Adventures in Wonderland*

Lewis Carroll (1865/2009)

Alice was beginning to get very tired of sitting by her sister on the bank, and having nothing to do:

So she was considering, in her own mind (as well as she could, for the hot day made her feel very sleepy and stupid) whether the pleasure of making a daisy-chain would be worth the trouble of getting up and picking the daisies, when suddenly a White Rabbit with pink eyes ran close by her.

. . . when the Rabbit actually *took a watch out of its waistcoat pocket*, and looked at it, and then hurried on, Alice started to her feet, for it flashed across her mind that she had never before seen a rabbit with either a waistcoat-pocket, or a watch to take out of it, and, burning with curiosity, she ran across the field after it, and was just in time to see it pop down a large rabbit-hole under the hedge.

In another moment down went Alice after it, never once considering how in the world she was to get out again.

(Carroll, 2009, pp. 9–10)

WHICH ALICE TO CHOOSE?

There are many different versions of Alice but I prefer the version abridged and illustrated by Tony Ross. The text has been considerably shortened but it loses none of the Victorian charm. And, of course, it is made all the better by the wonderful higgledy-piggledy illustrations by Tony Ross himself:

Alice's Adventures in Wonderland, Lewis Carroll, abridged and illustrated by Tony Ross (Anderson Press, 1993).

There is also a newer edition published by the same publisher in 2015.

This chapter is designed to give you lots of different investigations that will allow you to improve and assess the children's science skills. So, look out for the extra 'Science skills' boxes that will flag up which skills to focus on as you observe the class, listen to their reasoning and look at their work.

TOPIC PLANNER

Story link	Science Science skills	Activity	Page
Falling down the rabbit hole	Testing against a control Using one set of results to make predictions and set up further tests (Gravity and air resistance)	Designing parachutes (investigation)	185–6
Pool of tears	Estimating and predicting Taking repeat readings Plotting line graphs (Surface tension)	Teardrops on a penny (investigation)	192–3
The Rabbit sends in a Little Bill	Changing one variable and taking repeat readings (Push forces, gravity and air resistance)	Bill is kicked up the chimney (investigation)	196–7
Caterpillar bubbles	Setting up a comparative investigation (Bubbles)	Blowing the biggest bubble (investigation)	201
A mad tea party	Finding all the possible solutions Measuring accurately (Centre of gravity)	Topsy turvy cans (activity)	206–7
The rose garden	Planning an investigation and controlling variables Plotting bar charts and line graphs Paper absorbs by capillary action	Opening paper flowers (investigation)	212

FALLING DOWN THE RABBIT HOLE

Story link

The rabbit-hole went straight on like a tunnel for some way, and then dipped suddenly down, so suddenly that Alice had not a moment to think about stopping herself before she found herself falling down what seemed to be a very deep well.

(Carroll, 2009, p. 10)

THE SCIENCE: Gravity and air resistance

You can find the science of gravity and air resistance on p. 144 in *The Northern Lights* chapter. You may like to read that first in order to get to grips with the forces of gravity and air resistance.

When a parachute falls, the force of gravity is pulling it down towards the Earth. In the absence of air, the force of gravity would cause the parachutist to fall faster and faster, accelerating until the point at which the poor parachutist hit the ground and became pulp. Luckily for us, on Earth we have to fall through air particles. Each particle we bump into slows us down a little. If you imagine the air molecules acting like the plastic balls in a children's ball pit you can imagine how falling through the balls would slow you down as you bump into them.

If you have a small parachute, you will bump into some air particles and this air resistance will be significant enough to eventually stop you from accelerating any more. This is because the faster you fall the more air particles per second that you bump into. Or, to put it another way, air resistance increases in direct proportion to the increase in speed. The parachutist will eventually fall at a constant speed as the force of gravity will eventually be balanced by the air resistance. This is called terminal speed. However, with a small parachute, this constant speed (terminal speed) may well be too fast to survive the landing.

If you have a large parachute, there will be more air resistance from the point at which it starts to fall. This means that the parachutist will reach the point where the force of gravity is balanced by the air resistance earlier in the fall, and at a slower speed than the parachutist with a smaller parachute. The lucky skydiver with a large parachute, will hit the ground at a lower and safer speed and, with any luck, they will survive the landing.

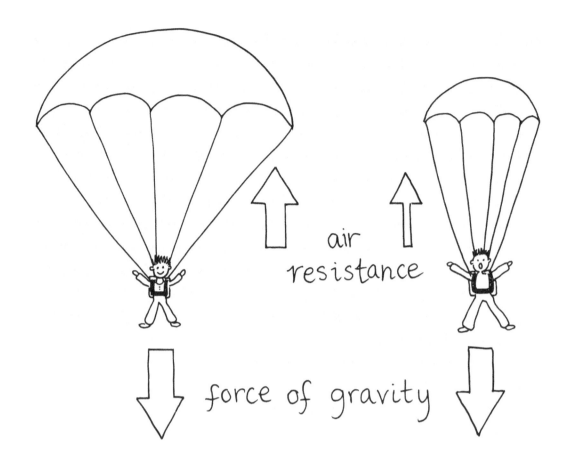

What do the children need to know?

The greater the functional surface area of the parachute, the more air resistance and the more slowly it will fall.

 INVESTIGATION: Designing parachutes

You will need:

- doll with billowy skirt
- thin paper or bin bags or basket-type coffee filters to make the parachutes (make sure you can cut it with school scissors)
- scissors

- tape
- embroidery thread – thicker than cotton, lighter than string (lots)
- plastic interlocking cubes (with hole for easy attachment to strings) or another small weight.

 Storify the science

Read Chapter 1 to the point where Alice lands in the hallway. Alice falls slowly. She thinks to herself that she will fall right through the centre of the Earth until she reaches the other side of the Earth where the people 'walk with their heads downwards'. Ask the children to discuss

Alice's ideas. Elicit the fact that it is the force of gravity that pulls you down. In fact, it pulls you towards the centre of the Earth so she couldn't fall right through. Once she got to the middle she would stop. They will probably also tell you that it is too hot in the centre of the Earth for a human to survive so even if she did fall to the centre she'd be incinerated!

However, in the book, Alice falls slowly. Ask what might the causes of this slowness be. They will give you all kinds of answers, all of which should be appreciated as this is set in a fictional world where anything is possible. However, if you have already studied forces, they will be familiar with the idea that, when you fall, you bump into air particles. They slow your fall and this is called air resistance.

Draw a forces diagram of Alice falling on the board. Ask where you should draw the air resistance acting. They will probably tell you that her skirt will billow out like a parachute and this will encounter air resistance.

Continue with this idea. How big would her skirt have to be to make her fall really slowly?

Drop a doll with a billowy skirt. Note that it hits the ground with quite a bang. Ask whether the doll landed safely. She didn't!

The doll may even topple over and hit the ground head first. Discuss how you could make sure that your feet hit the ground first by using the skirt above your head as a parachute, i.e. lowering your centre of gravity so that you are no longer top heavy and liable to tip over.

The following activity is designed to focus on the following science skills: testing against a control and using one set of results to make predictions and set up further tests.

Ideally, you need to let the children learn all about parachutes by making one as the control and getting it to work by tinkering with it. Then ask them to make a test parachute that is larger. Once they have seen the effect of changing the size they can try even larger or even smaller depending what they want to try. They should predict what they think will happen each time and test it to see whether they are correct.

 ## Set the challenge

You are going to investigate falling slowly. You will investigate the effect of changing the size of a parachute on the speed at which the parachutists falls. In order to model this in the classroom we need to work with smaller models so your parachutist will be a small plastic cube.

First, make a control parachute. We can then make changes to the design and make a new parachute – a test parachute. Then, we can test it to see whether it falls faster or more slowly than our control parachute. After that, you can decide what your third parachute will be and, if you have time, your fourth!

When you design your test parachute, think about:

• which variable you will change;

• which variables you will have to keep the same in order to make your test fair;

• what you will measure to show which falls fastest.

When you test your parachutes, think about:

- how many times you will carry out the test to be sure that the results are repeatable and not just a fluke;
- how to make the test as fair as possible;
- what you want to try next and what you think will happen with the next one.

What did you find out about parachutes?

 ## Teacher's top tips

The exact template doesn't matter as long as you use the same material and shape each time. A simple square of bin bag with tread tied or taped to each corner works well as the bin bag plastic is sufficiently thin and flexible to create a dome shape. The circular coffee filters work

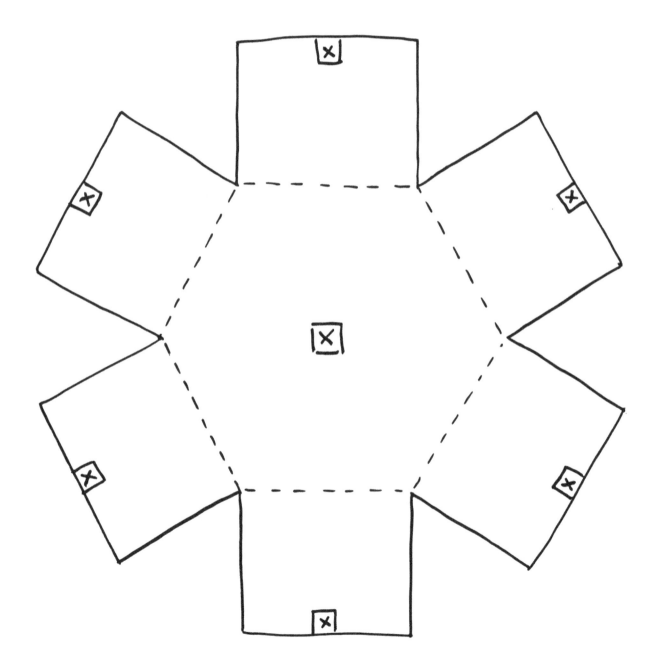

well but could be expensive and you wouldn't be able to make larger ones but you could make smaller ones by cutting them down. You could also use a hexagonal based design as shown, with a thread attached to the middle or side of each flap. A plastic cube is usually a good item to tie on the bottom to act as the parachutist.

Take care to make the threads of equal length. The square bin bag design is easier to work with as the plastic domes and small differences in the length of the threads don't affect the canopy shape much or send them wildly off course. The flatter, paper designs need fairly exact thread lengths or the cube hangs to one side and the parachute goes off course.

If you have a balcony or other safe platform from which to drop the parachutes then it is best to use that rather than have children standing on chairs in the classroom. If you have no other alternative, check the Health and Safety requirements at your establishment before asking children to climb on chairs to launch their parachutes and insist that great care is taken.

You can tape a small piece of paper to the centre of the uppermost surface of the parachute canopy as a handle to hold it by, during the launch.

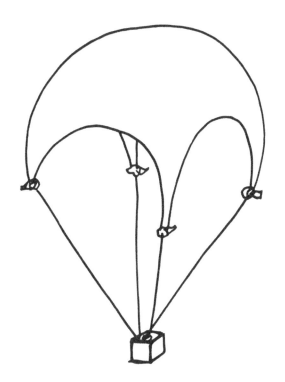
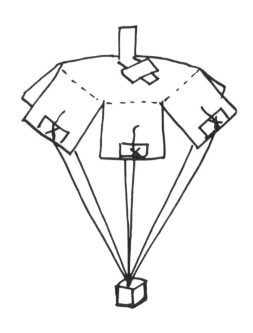

What results should I expect?

Keeping all other factors the same, the larger the surface area of the parachute canopy, the slower it should fall.

If you want to plot a line graph of results, you will need to know the area of the canopy and measure the time taken to fall. To make this easy, use squared paper to create the canopy. It does yield a nice line graph and you can predict intermediate values from the graph, then test them to see whether they are accurate, i.e. if you know the time taken for a parachute with a canopy of 25 cm squared and one with a canopy of 75 cm squared, you can estimate the time taken for a parachute with a canopy of 50 cm squared, using the graph you have plotted.

Finale

Show children pictures of a real parachutist. Note the enormous size of the parachute compared to the person hanging below it. Return to the topic of Alice. Could it be her skirt that is slowing her down? Would that work? Conclude that it is a work of fiction and that the rules of physics don't apply in stories! Her skirt would have to be enormous and she'd have to hang below it, making it a most impractical outfit.

 What next?

If you want to record your findings in a creative way then you could:

- Draw a picture of Alice in a ridiculously oversized skirt and annotate the drawing with forces arrows to explain the forces involved in Alice falling slowly.

- Design a parachute for Alice, complete with instructions on how to use it and an explanation of how it works, just in case she falls down any rabbit holes in the future.

- Write a scientific news article about Alice falling down the rabbit hole, explaining why you think the entire rabbit hole episode must have been a dream by pointing out the scientific flaws in her account.

 Assessing children's understanding

The following statements are indicators of basic understanding:

- The force of gravity pulls a parachutist (or Alice) down to the centre of the Earth.
- Larger parachutes fall more slowly than small ones (if everything but the size of the canopy is kept the same).
- The larger canopies bump into more air so there is more air resistance.
- Air resistance makes you fall more slowly.

More advanced understanding:

- Without air, the force of gravity keeps on pulling on falling objects so they accelerate towards the ground.
- Air resistance gets bigger as you move faster through air because you bump into more air molecules per second.
- There is a point where a falling object stops accelerating and falls at a constant speed towards the ground because the force of gravity is now balanced by the greater air resistance. This is terminal speed.

Patterns they may be able to describe:

- The larger the effective surface area of the canopy, the slower the parachute will fall.

Science skills

Remember to look out for evidence of **testing against a control and using one set of results to make predictions and set up further tests**.

In this experiment, you will be encouraging them to test their own design against their original parachute (their control), so just make sure all children are dropping two parachutes at a time to race them or measuring time taken to fall for the control parachute and their own design. Then they can compare the two to see which falls more slowly.

You can also listen out for children who are making observations about one parachute and asking whether they can try something out, based on what they observed. You can always help them to predict by asking what they think will happen. Then, let them test all the ideas you are able to safely test in the classroom.

THE POOL OF TEARS

Story link

... she soon made out that she was in the pool of tears which she had wept when she was nine feet high. 'I wish I hadn't cried so much!' said Alice, as she swam about, trying to find her way out. 'I shall be punished for it now, I suppose, by being drowned in my own tears!'

(Carroll, 2009, pp. 70-1)

THE SCIENCE: Surface tension

Due to the way in which the molecules in a liquid are bonded, an elastic-like film is produced where the liquid is in contact with the air – this is called surface tension. Water has a particularly high surface tension. The surface tension in water is large enough for it to form small droplets/tears or to allow pond skaters to walk across its surface. It is surface tension that causes droplets on a glass surface to form a dome of water that sticks up well above the surface it is standing upon.

INVESTIGATION: Teardrops on a penny

You will need:

- one pence coins (or another small coin)
- two pence coins (or another larger coin)
- other coins of different sizes
- pipettes
- pots of water.

 ## Storify the science

Read Chapter 2. Ask the children what would happen if they cried giant tears on the floor. If you are sitting on a carpet at the time then they may tell you that the tears would all sink in.

If there is a wooden or plastic floor covering, they may be able to describe how the droplets would sit in little dome shapes on the floor. Take a pipette and drip a tear sized drop of water on the desk in front of them and ask them to describe what they see. Imagine what it might look like if you were only an inch high. If you have a hand-held digital microscope, show the children a close-up image of the droplet so they can see what it would look like to tiny Alice.

Discuss the way the water domes. Introduce the idea that you are going to look at pools of water. Demonstrate how to drip one drop from a pipette. You might need to give them time to practise this.

 ## Set the challenge

You are going to use the pipettes to cry yourself a pool of tears on this penny coin. Look carefully at the coin. Estimate how many drips will fit on the coin. Write this number down as an estimate.

Drip the drops one at a time. Observe carefully and count the number of drips.

Was your estimate accurate? Close? Miles off?

Repeat the experiment until you are sure you have a repeatable answer.

Now look carefully at the two pence coin. Estimate how many drips will fit on this larger coin. Write this number down as an estimate.

Repeat the experiment until you are sure you have a repeatable answer.

Choose a different coin with a different diameter.

Make a prediction and repeat the experiment.

Draw a line graph to show the relationship between the diameter coin and the number of drops you can fit on it.

Extension

If you have time, try adding a drop of washing up liquid to the water and repeating the penny experiment. How many drips on a penny now?

 ## Teacher's top tips

Encourage the children to repeat the experiment until they get the same result (or nearly) a few times so they are sure that they have carried the experiment out accurately.

Place your penny on kitchen towel or newspaper to avoid flooding the table.

It works best on a really flat surface with clean, dry coins.

Use this opportunity to revise the diameter of the circles and to plot the graph and use it to find intermediate values.

Do spend some time explaining surface tension and relate it to the way pond skaters move across the surface of the water. You could even float paperclips on the water. To do this you need to float the paperclip on tissue first then gently ease the tissue away. There are plenty of videos of this on the internet.

What results should I expect?

You can get about 36 drips on a penny. It domes up a long way before the surface tension breaks.

The washing up liquid reduces the surface tension so that it forms smaller droplets. The number of drips on the same penny will be different with soapy water.

 ## What next?

If you want to record your findings in a creative way then you could:

* Research surface tension. Find out why you can get so many teardrops on a penny. Write a little book on surface tension for all the creatures in Wonderland. Some creatures, such as pond skaters, even use surface tension to walk on water. You could explain how this wondrous feat is achieved without magic.

* Role-play: being little inch-high Alice telling her nine foot counterpart to stop crying and describe the droplets as they begin to form pools on the ground. Explain why the drips make little domes of deep water before they spread out across the floor.

* Write a formal letter of complaint to the owner of the hallway, explaining that the wooden floor is very dangerous for small creatures, in the presence of very large and lachrymose ones (tearful) as the water tends to form domes that can be too deep for small creatures. Make sure you explain the science behind it. Campaign for carpet in the hallway (short piled) for the safety of all small creatures.

* Write a lab report of the experiment and explain why you need to repeat the experiment.

Assessing children's understanding

The following statements are indicators of basic understanding:

- The water doesn't lie flat on the surface of the penny. It domes.
- Roughly the same number of drops fit on the penny each time.
- I need to repeat my experiment to check my results are not a fluke.

More advanced understanding:

- The water domes because the molecules on the outer surface of the water droplet stick together. This is surface tension.
- If I repeat my experiment and get the same results, I know that those results are valid and not a fluke.

Patterns they may be able to describe:

- The greater the diameter of the coin, the greater the number of droplets that will fit on the coin.

Science skills

Remember to look out for evidence of **estimating, predicting, taking repeat readings and plotting line graphs**.

It will be easy to assess their ability to draw line graphs as you'll spot the children who struggle and note the more capable by the confidence with which they approach the task and the quality of the graph they produce. Make sure you ask some questions about the graph so you know they can interpret it too.

Have a class discussion on how many times you should repeat the experiment and you can make a group decision on the number.

If you ask the children to predict everything at the start of the investigation, their estimating won't improve based on the results of the first experiment. So, ask them to predict immediately before each test so they can enjoy being more accurate each time.

THE RABBIT SENDS IN A LITTLE BILL

Story link

She drew her foot as far down the chimney as she could, and waited till she heard a little animal (she couldn't guess of what sort it was) scratching and scrambling about in the chimney close above her: then, saying to herself 'This is Bill', she gave one sharp kick, and waited to see what would happen next.

(Carroll, 2009, p. 35)

THE SCIENCE: Push forces, gravity and air resistance

In this activity, a small paper model of Little Bill is fired upwards by a jet of air in much the same way as a stomp rocket. The activity is based on 'Rocket Mice' which can be found on the Science Museum (London) website. My thanks go to the Science Museum for letting me include their design. The mouse is, in essence, a small paper cone. A soft plastic milk bottle beneath the mouse is compressed by a child's hands. If this is done at speed, the air in the bottle is forced out of the neck of the bottle and anything placed over the neck of the bottle will be pushed upwards.

The science of the mouse moving upwards is fairly simple. Hands push on the bottle, the bottle pushes on the air inside causing it to come out of the top and the mouse, positioned over the top of the bottle, is pushed upwards. Gravity is pulling the mouse down but the push force is sufficiently large to overcome the effect of gravity and the mouse moves upwards.

Once the air has stopped pushing the mouse, it will continue upwards but get slower until it reaches a standstill. While it is in this slowing down (deceleration) phase, gravity is pulling on the mouse back down to Earth and air resistance is acting upon the mouse too, slowing its progress upwards. The part the children find hard to understand is that the air is no longer pushing the mouse at this point. The only forces at play are air resistance and gravity.

From now on, the mouse will play the part of Little Bill.

INVESTIGATION: Bill is kicked up the chimney

You will need:

- a variety of plastic bottles – the largest size of supermarket milk bottles work best but provide all the varieties you can drink your way through and have fizzy drink bottles in all shapes and sizes available too. Aim to provide at least one bottle per child

- photocopies of the 'Rocket Mice' template from The Science Museum's website

- enlarged and reduced photocopies of the template

- scissors

- glue sticks.

 Storify the science

Read Chapter 4 up to the part where Alice manages to kick Little Bill right up and out of the chimney. Ask the children which forces are involved.

Once they have given you some ideas, begin to separate the process into parts: Little Bill is being kicked, Little Bill is moving upwards and Little Bill is falling down again. Draw these parts as a diagram. Ask the children where you should draw the forces arrows.

Elicit that the kick can only act on Little Bill while he is contact with Alice's foot. Draw this force on the first diagram.

After this, Little Bill is moving upwards but he is slowing down as gravity and air resistance pull him in the opposite direction. Draw these forces only on the next diagram. It is a common misconception to think that the kick is still pushing Bill up at this point. Show that it is not, as the foot is no longer in contact with Bill.

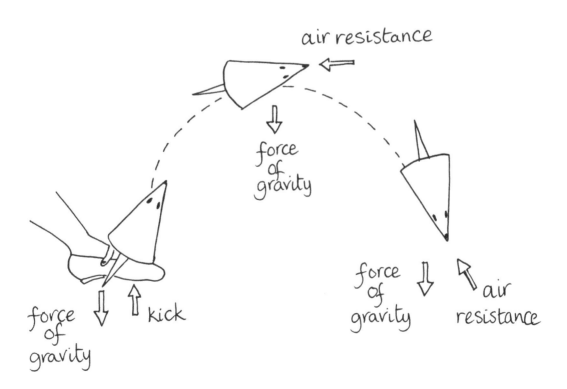

Finally, elicit that when Little Bill is moving downwards, air resistance will slow his fall by acting upwards now while the force of gravity continues to pull Little Bill down.

Introduce the idea that you are going to investigate ways to make Bill go higher in the air by changing different variables.

Explain that instead of kicking Little Bill into the air we will use a safer method involving air. Show the equipment and demonstrate how to roll the paper into a cone, add a tail and launch it.

 ## Set the challenge

You are going to make a model of Little Bill who was a lizard. Use the 'Rocket Mice' template to form a paper cone that will fit over the neck of a plastic milk bottle.

Add a small paper tail to your cone to make it more lizard-like. Balance your Little Bill model on the neck of the plastic milk bottle (like a hat – pointy end upwards) and clap your hands forcefully together on either side of the bottle to violently push in the sides of the bottle. Your Little Bill model should shoot upwards.

Think about all the different things that you could change about this launching process. Make a list of them.

Now, change one variable while keeping all the others the same.

Does it make a difference to how high Little Bill goes?

Once you have repeated the test enough times to be sure of the result, choose another variable to investigate.

 ## Teacher's top tips

First, let them play.

Playing will help them to understand what is going on by having first-hand experience of the science. They will be much more likely to be able to list the variables that might make a difference to the height Little Bill goes, when they have had a go themselves.

Collect a class list of possible variables they could alter.

Once they have played, they will be ready to tinker. It is nigh on impossible to hit the bottle the same every time so these will never be truly fair tests. But you can encourage observation, testing and manipulating the equipment to find ways to improve the height Little Bill flies. This is what I would call tinkering! Encourage the children to change one thing at a time so they know what is making the difference.

It is hard to compare the height of the flight when Little Bill hits the ceiling all the time. And without a slo-mo camera you'll be hard pushed to measure the height it travels. So, you may wish to find a way to prop the bottle at an angle and then Little Bill can travel along the classroom, rather than upwards and you can measure the distance travelled. You'll have to ensure a tight fit of the bottom of the cone shape onto the top of the bottle in order to prevent it falling off before launch.

Hard plastic cola bottles tend not to work as well as the softer milk bottles but provide all kinds as this is a great variable to investigate and they can't **choose** the right one if there are no wrong choices to discount.

What results should I expect?

There some variables that have obvious effects:

- Hitting the bottle harder makes Little Bill fly higher.
- Bigger bottles have more air in them so they tend to give more of a push.
- Softer plastics will bend more easily so more air is pushed out of the bottle.
- The seal created by the base of the cone on the neck of the bottle has a big effect so fitting the cone to the neck of the bottle will help.

Other variables may give interesting effects:

- Large additions to Little Bill (e.g. a hat) tend to make him less aerodynamic and he won't fly so well.
- Adding a little weight to the nose of the cone can make a difference.

 ## What next?

If you want to record your findings in a creative way then you could:

- Role–play: a press conference where Alice and Little Bill are interviewed about their behaviour and their motives. Be sure to have a scientific editor available to comment on what happened and explain to the press why Alice's behaviour was so dangerous.
- Write a scientific report of what happened. Make sure you include diagrams showing the forces and interviews with a scientist who can explain what happened.
- Create a slo-mo film of Little Bill (by filming the actual experiment or by acting it out in slow motion). Then, using a film making app (such as iMovies) add a voice-over to the video images. You could be in role as a sport commentator, pointing out the forces at play during each part of the process. Use diagrams where possible.
- Write instructions for Alice on how to get Little Bill to go as high as possible in this experiment with the cone and the milk bottle.

 ## Assessing children's understanding

The following statements are indicators of basic understanding:

- When I hit the bottle hard, Little Bill flies up a long way.
- The air coming out of the bottle is pushing Little Bill up.
- The force of gravity pulls Little Bills down again.
- If Little Bill has parts that stick out they bump into air particles. This causes air resistance so Bill doesn't fly so far.

More advanced understanding:

- All the air in the bottle has to fit through the neck of the bottle so it comes out of the neck very fast creating a strong push force.
- When Little Bill is going up but no longer being pushed by the air, the only forces acting on it are air resistance and the force of gravity.

Patterns they may be able to describe:

- The harder you whack the bottle, the higher Little Bill goes.
- The better the seal of the cone on the bottle neck, the higher Little Bill goes.
- The more streamlined the model of Little Bill is, the further he will fly as there is less air resistance.

Science skills

Remember to look out for evidence of **changing one variable and taking repeat readings**.

A good way to check they understand how to change one variable at a time is to ask them to write down which one they are changing and then a list of all the variables they will keep the same.

Again, have a class discussion about how many times you should repeat the test in order to be sure that the result is repeatable and not a fluke. Agree, as a class, on an appropriate number and spend time explaining that this is not linked to making the test fair. It is about making sure that a particular result is not a fluke and that the same result can be obtained by repeating the same test.

In this test, there are lots of variables that are hard to control, so spend time working out what might make the results different each time.

———————————

CATERPILLAR BUBBLES

Story link

She stretched herself up on tiptoe, and peeped over the edge of the mushroom, and her eyes immediately met those of a large blue caterpillar, that was sitting on the top, with its arms folded, quietly smoking a long hookah, and taking not the smallest notice of her or of anything else.

(Carroll, 2009, p. 39)

THE SCIENCE: Bubbles

Bubbles are made when air (or another gas) is trapped inside a thin layer of soapy water. The soap forms a skin on the inside and the outside that sandwich a layer of water between them. When the water dries up the bubble pops. So, if the bubble lands on anything dry it will pop.

Bubbles are round (once you have detached them from the bubble wand) because the surface tension of the soapy water is pulling the bubble inwards and the smallest volume it can occupy is a sphere.

Amazingly, a bubble wall is very thin, even thinner than a human hair. Bubble walls can range from 10–1000 nanometres, whereas a hair is 40 000 to 60 000 nanometres thick.

INVESTIGATION: Blowing the biggest bubble

You will need:

- clean straws
- pots of water (ideally these should be deep and transparent so bubbles can be observed)
- pipe cleaners
- good bubble mix (recipes can be found on the internet)
- pots for the bubble mix
- hoops
- large trays for the bubble mix
- large outdoor area or slip-proof, waterproof floor.

Storify the science

Read the end of Chapter 4 and into the start of Chapter 5 where Alice encounters the caterpillar. The caterpillar is smoking a hookah pipe. At this point, emphasise that when this story was written, the harmful effects of smoking were not known. Point out that you don't find smoking in children's books nowadays. However, these particular pipes are quite interesting as they make bubbles.

Give the children clean straws and ask them to blow into water. Ask them to try to make different sized bubbles, one at a time. Let them observe the bubbles they are making. If they work in pairs, encourage one to watch while the other blows the bubbles. If you blow gently you can make smaller bubbles. If you blow hard you can blow lots of small bubbles that join up to make a bigger one on the way to the surface.

Now show them a standard, shop-bought, pot of bubble mix and a wand and blow some bubbles. Explain that they are going to try making bubbles of their own. Show them how to shape a pipe cleaner into a bubble wand. Use something such as a board marker to wind the pipe cleaner around to make a bubble wand that is about 2 cm in diameter.

Go outside and let them try blowing bubbles. Talk about all the things they notice. Look at the film inside the bubble wand. Look at the rainbows and reflections on the surface. Try catching bubbles.

 ## Set the challenge

You are going to try making different sized bubbles. Try to make very big bubbles and very small bubbles. Can you make different shaped bubbles?

Think about:

- how you blow;
- the shape of your bubble wand;
- the size of your bubble wand.

What did you find out about bubbles?

 ## Teacher's top tips

Let the children play first.

Eventually, someone will try making a larger bubble wand and the pattern here is the larger the bubble wand the larger the bubbles. But don't prompt it. Let the children have enough time to work it out for themselves. Eventually, someone will ask if they can make a bigger one.

They will also be able to increase the size of the bubble by blowing gently and steadily before releasing the bubble but they'll make even bigger ones doing the same thing with a bigger wand.

With larger bubble wands, you'll need to swing the wand through the air to fill the bubble up rather than blowing.

Once the bubbles are released, they will all end up spherical. The children may enjoy working this out by trying different shaped bubbles wands.

This is important . . . **Make your own mixture!** Find a good mixture from the internet – the best ones contain added glycerine or lubricant. The mixture you can buy in the shop won't be as good as these.

Work outside if you can, on a non-slip surface such as grass or asphalt. Avoid working in rooms with shiny floors that will become slippery if the mixture is spilled.

If you want to appear to be a real expert (or have magical powers) follow the advice of the bubble lady, Sarah Bearchell (*Sarah's Adventures in Science*). She says, this is the way to spot when a bubble is about to pop:

When the wall is thick on a new bubble, you get a pure reflection from the outer surface, so you see the sky and trees etc.

When it thins a bit, you get the coloured interference patterns as the light is reflected off the inner and outer walls differently.

Then, the wall thins and seems to go black. This happens just before it pops. So, when you see it go black you know it is about to pop and you can predict it and look really clever!

 Finale

You can make a giant bubble using a decent mix (find one on the internet) and a large plastic hula hoop in a large tray of bubble mix. You can even stand inside it while you raise the hoop

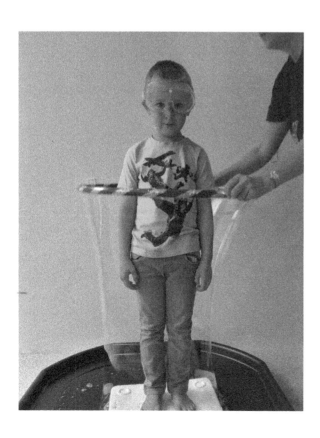 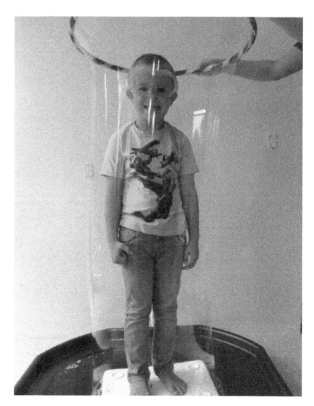

up around you. Have a go at this before you try it with the children and take plenty of photographs.

The Royal Institution have also developed a great tool for making bubbles that is made from string tied to two wooden spoons and a weight. You hold the spoons in your hands and dangle the weight on the string between the spoons making a big triangular string loop for your wand. Then, you can wave the contraption to catch the air and make giant bubbles. There's a great video of it in action on their website at the time of writing.

What results should I expect?

The larger the bubble wand the bigger the bubble!

And . . . the more mixture that is spilled, the slippier the floor. So, do remember to do this outside on grass or asphalt.

What next?

If you want to record your findings in a creative way then you could:

- Write a report for the caterpillar on how you made the biggest bubble.
- Role-play: being a bubble expert and explain how to make bubbles of different sizes. Write the script for a documentary on bubbles.
- Role-play: a conversation between the Caterpillar and Alice where the Caterpillar asks Alice all kinds of questions about bubbles and Alice has to answer them.
- Create a mini-book all about bubbles for the people of Wonderland.

Assessing children's understanding

The following statements are indicators of basic understanding:

- Bubbles are made when pockets of air are trapped inside the soapy water.
- Bubbles are always round, even if the bubble wand is not.
- To make a big bubble you need a big bubble wand (and a good bubble mixture).

More advanced understanding:

- Bubbles are made because the molecules in the soapy water cling together. This is called surface tension.
- Bubbles are always round because the surface tension presses the air into the smallest volume and the shape this creates is a sphere.

Patterns they may be able to describe:

- The bigger the wand, the bigger bubble you can make.

Science skills

Remember to look out for evidence of **setting up a comparative investigation**.

It isn't possible to measure anything as transitory as a bubble (without really clever equipment) so the children are merely comparing in this activity. It cannot easily be done as a fair test but it is possible to note the general patterns. All they really need to do is to come up with two or more bubble wands to compare and note the difference between the bubbles they produce. I would suggest, for most children, this is the very least they would do in this investigation so it should be easy to note any children who struggle to do this.

Thanks to Sarah Bearchell – the bubble lady – (*Sarah's Adventures in Science*) for her help with this chapter and for her photographs of the lovely Archie (Copyright Sarah Bearchell, 2004).

A MAD TEA PARTY

Story link

There was a table set out under a tree in front of the house, and the March Hare and the Hatter were having tea at it: a Dormouse was sitting between them, fast asleep, and the other two were using it as a cushion, resting their elbows on it, and talking over its head. 'Very uncomfortable for the Dormouse,' thought Alice; ' only, as it's asleep, I suppose it doesn't mind.'

The table was a large one, but the three were all crowded together at one corner of it. 'No room! No room!' they cried out when they saw Alice coming. 'There's plenty of room!' said Alice indignantly, and she sat down in a large arm-chair at one end of the table.

(Carroll, 2009, p. 60)

THE SCIENCE: Centre of gravity

This is the place on an object where gravity appears to act.

As humans, our centre of gravity is somewhere in our middles, below our stomach but over our hips. When we stand up straight our centre is directly over our feet so we can stay upright easily. Imagine standing on a moving bus. It's hard to remain upright when the bus lurches and tips us forwards or backwards. If we lean over to one side, our centre of gravity is no longer over our feet and it will tend to be pulled to the floor by the force of gravity, so we fall over.

Now imagine a tall pole made of wood. If you tried to stand it upright, it would be really hard to get it to stay up. This is because the centre of gravity is half way up the wooden pole and that's a long way up. It is easy to put the centre of gravity off centre and send the pole crashing down.

Now imagine the bottom third of the pole is made of something really dense and heavy such as lead or concrete. Now there is more mass at the bottom so the centre of gravity is lower. It is harder to get the centre of gravity over to one side so the pole is more stable.

Buses don't tip over, despite being quite tall, because their centre of gravity is not halfway up the bus, it is much lower due to the weight of the engine at the bottom of the bus. Sports cars don't tip because they are low to the ground so their centre of gravity is low as well.

ACTIVITY: Topsy turvy cans

You will need:

- empty Coca Cola cans (branded) – enough for one per pair of children
- other empty coke cans (various brands, volumes and can designs)
- beakers full of water
- trays to avoid spillages
- empty measuring beakers.

Storify the science

Read the whole of Chapter 7. Ask the children how a tea party like that would make you feel. Elicit that it is chaotic and confusing and the rules keep changing etc.

Now ask them to suggest the menu for a mad tea party of their own. When one of them suggests a fizzy drink, get out your can of coke (already filled with 100 ml of water) and, without drawing attention to what you are doing, balance it on the desk on one corner, as shown overleaf.

This should get a reaction. Now pay close attention to the can and ask the children what seems odd about it. Give a child an empty can or a full unopened can and ask them to try – it will tip over. Ask them to suggest how it might be possible. Eventually, someone will suggest that there is something inside the can and someone may then suggest this is water.

Don't let them see how much water is in your can, remove it and get started straight away, while they are still curious.

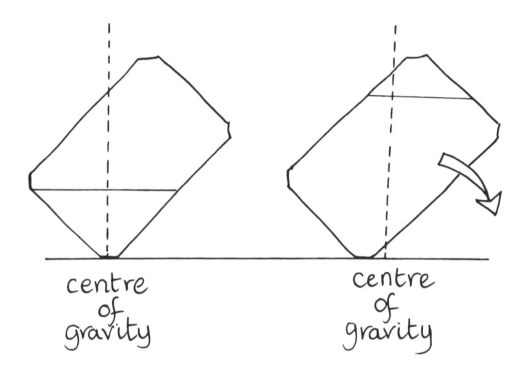

centre
of
gravity

centre
of
gravity

 ## Set the challenge

You are going to try to balance your coke can in the same way.

Think about these questions.

- How can you get it to balance?
- What is going on inside?
- Is there only one answer?

 ## Teacher's top tips

Work on trays – it will get messy while they try.

Provide a range of coke cans so they can try with all of them. The mini cans you get on aeroplanes are not bevelled in the same way and won't sit on one corner.

When they have made it work once, ask them if they can make it work with a different amount of water.

Once they realise that the amount of water can vary and it still works, ask them to find the minimum amount of water it takes to make the can balance on one edge, and the maximum.

Ask the children to explain what is going on – they could draw diagrams like the ones above.

What results should I expect?

This will vary according to the can design but you can make a Coca Cola can stand on one edge with as little as 40 ml of water in it and as much as 220 ml.

When the can has equal mass on either side of the corner where it is balanced the centre of gravity remains in the middle. When the shape of the can dictates that more mass is on one side, then the centre of gravity is off centre and the can will topple over.

 ## Finale

Prepare a cake tin, in advance, with a 100 g mass (or a stone) taped to the inside edge as shown. Place the lid on and make sure you know where the mass is taped. Set up a ramp on the desk and place the tin onto the centre of the ramp. Set your cake tin with the weight at the top but just slightly off centre towards the uphill side of the ramp.

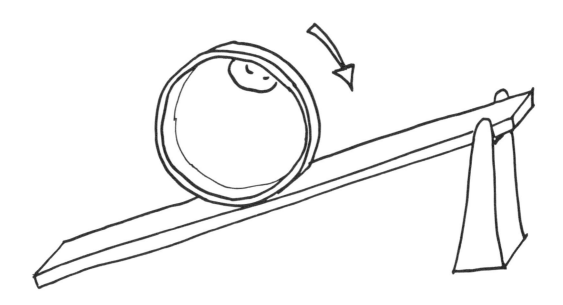

Ask the children what will happen when you let go. They will assume the tin will roll down the ramp. However, as you let go, the force of gravity will pull the heavy mass down and this will make the tin roll up hill.

Repeat this until the children begin to suggest there is something inside the tin. Don't reveal it until they have worked out where the weight must be. Pretend to be innocent and that it is magic up until the point where they work it out.

If the cake tin slips on the ramp, stretch thick elastic bands around the tin to act as a non-slip surface to grip the ramp.

Relate the science back to the experiment they have just done. If the centre of gravity is off to one side, it will roll until the mass is in the centre at the bottom. You can use this to make it roll uphill.

Alternative finale!

Fix a large brightly coloured helium balloon conveniently near where you will be speaking. Walk in with a large cardboard box (apparently very heavy) and hold it on the edge of a table, ensuring that the box can be seen to project a long way over the edge of the table.

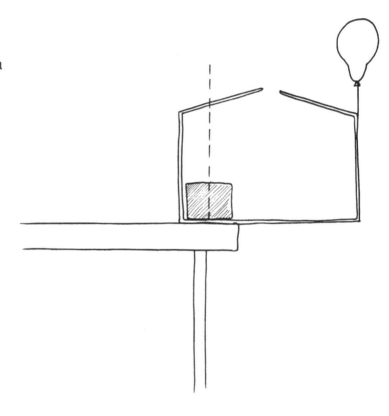

Ask a child to attach the balloon to the end of the box away from the table. Let go of the box, which stays in place because there is a brick inside it, in the part that is on the table.

Ask whether the box will fall if the balloon is removed. Once they have discussed this, ask a child to remove the balloon and show that the box is still balanced. Finally, after discussion, you might show them the brick.

 ## What next?

If you want to record your findings in a creative way then you could:

- Set up a mad tea party for a guest and show off your new balancing can trick. Then, wow them with your scientific knowledge by explaining what is going on, while you help them to get the trick to work for themselves. You could even combine this with other tea party themed tricks, such as the cake tin rolling uphill and the pulling the tablecloth out from under the tea-set.

- Write a step-by-step set of instructions of how to set up these tricks, with diagrams at every stage to explain what is going on. You could design the booklet for one of the guests at the Mad Hatter's tea party and call it 'How to Host a Mad Tea Party'.
- Write the script for a TV show called 'How do you do that?' Include the dialogue for two presenters – one who does the trick in role as the Mad Hatter and one who is in role as a scientist, explaining what is going on. Then perform it and create your own show!

 ## Assessing children's understanding

The following statements are indicators of basic understanding:

- The can will balance on one edge when I put a bit of water in it.

More advanced understanding:

- The can will balance when the mass on each side is the same. If you put too much water into the can there will be more mass on one side because of the shape of the can, so it overbalances.
- The centre of gravity has to be over the corner of the can in order to balance on that corner.

Science skills

Remember to look out for evidence of children **finding the all the possible solutions** and those who can **measure accurately.**

The more accurate measurers will be able to refine a particular range to the nearest 5 ml. I like to let the first child who thinks they have the answer put the maximum amount of water and the minimum of water on the board. Then if anyone decides the maximum is larger or the minimum is smaller, they write their measurement next to it until we are down to the nearest ml. At this point, you can check their measurements for accuracy and agree on a range for a particular variety of can. And you'll have a list of the names of children (on the board) who measured accurately and found the range easily!

THE ROSE GARDEN

Story link

A large rose-tree stood near the entrance of the garden: the roses growing on it were white, but there were three gardeners at it, busily painting them red.

(Carroll, 2009, p. 69)

THE SCIENCE: paper absorbs water by capillary action

Paper is made from wood fibres. Wood fibres are made of cellulose molecules that are a series of sugar molecules, bonded together in one long chain.

When you place one end of an absorbent paper into water, the water will soak into the paper that is in the water. It will also absorb into the paper above the water line. It is moving upwards against gravity, which is impressive. This process is called capillary action.

The water moves into the spaces between the cellulose fibres and, little by little, the molecules of water are attracted to, and move towards, the cellulose fibres.

As liquids are loosely bonded to one another, the liquid molecules stay together so if one moves upwards towards some cellulose, it pulls the rest with it. Thus, the liquid gradually creeps upwards into the paper in the tiny spaces between the fibres.

The water also breaks up the cellulose and weakens the structure of the fibres so that wet paper is much weaker than dry.

In this experiment, we see folded paper unfold when water is absorbed by the paper. This happens because the paper swells up with the water it has absorbed and where the paper is folded it expands and therefore unfolds! You can demonstrate this, in the classroom, with an empty balloon that is folded in half. When you make the balloon fill with air and expand, the balloon unfolds.

INVESTIGATION: Opening paper flowers

You will need:

- a rose or a photograph of a rose
- large trays of water
- scissors

- different sized 2D circular items to draw around (milk bottle or jam-jar lids will do)
- a variety of papers from A4 photocopier paper to sugar paper (incl. red), e.g. newspaper, shiny magazine paper, greaseproof paper, other colours of sugar paper (as they vary in absorbency)
- plenty of absorbent towels to dry desks!
- hand-held digital microscope
- timers.

This activity is based on the Japanese art of Kirigami where paper is folded and cut to make 3D shapes. You can find lots of YouTube demonstrations of this investigation by searching the internet for 'opening paper flowers in water'. You can even find templates and extra ideas.

 ## Storify the science

Read the last paragraph of Chapter 7 and then move on to Chapter 8. Alice has finally reached the garden. Ask the children why the gardeners are painting the roses red. Elicit that they planted the wrong plants in the first place. Ask why the gardeners couldn't tell the colour of the roses when they planted them. Elicit that the petals are only revealed when the roses bloom. Show them a real rose. Spend time talking about the names for all the parts. Show how the sepals protect the delicate petals until they are ready to open.

Cut out a white paper flower (A4 photocopy paper) and fold in one petal at a time, following the instructions below. Cut another flower of the same size and shape from red sugar paper and fold it in the same way. There are flower templates overleaf. You will also need a tray of water, at least an inch deep.

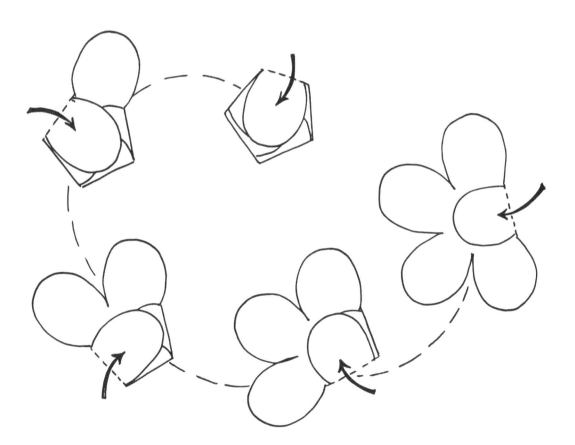

Show them the flowers and tell them you are going to drop them in the water. Ask them what they think might happen. Accept all answers from float/sink to dissolve, without revealing which is right.

Drop the white one into the water, folded petal side up. It should open quite slowly. It usually gets a good reaction as the petals open.

Ask what they think will happen with the red one. Answers will probably be more accurate now! Now drop the red one into the water. This one should open much faster as sugar paper absorbs water much faster than high quality photocopier paper.

Ask the children which one was fastest and how they could prove it. (You could time them or race one against another by dropping them in at the same time.)

If you are feeling ambitious, prepare one with two layers. Cut and fold a small red sugar paper flower. Cut a larger green sugar paper flower and cut a small hole in the centre. Place the folded red flower in the centre of the green one and fold petals of the green one over the red, concealing it.

Reveal this green flower last of all. Ask the children what colour this rose is. They will likely say green. When you place this in the water you should get a good reaction as the green one opens to reveal the red then the red one opens.

Let the children make one flower and try putting it on the water before you set the challenge. They will have far more ideas about what to try once they have had a go.

Set the challenge

You are going to investigate which variables make the flower open more quickly.

When you design your test think about:

- all the variables you could choose to change;
- which variable you will change;
- which variables you must keep the same;
- how you will measure which is fastest.

Which flower opened fastest? Can you explain why?

 ## Teacher's top tips

Let the children play first.

Once they have tried a few, they'll be ready to suggest a list of variables they could test. These include:

- size of flower (draw around the larger circular items to draw the centre of large flowers);
- number of petals;
- type of paper;
- number of layers (where one flower is inside another).

They will find it hard to keep all the other variables the same while they are changing one so you may want to have a set of templates. I often provide a couple of printed sheets with the same flower in different sizes as shown on the facing page.

Whip out the opened paper flowers quickly and recycle them as they will get in the way if left in the water tray.

Be on hand to cut flowers for less able children. Even at age ten, not all children can cut accurately.

If you want to draw graphs with the data, you will need to measure how long it takes a flower to open on a timer. Data such as different types of paper or number of petals can then be plotted on a bar chart. You cannot use a line graph for type of paper because the data is discontinuous – there is no midpoint between blue paper and red paper.

To collect data to be presented on a line graph you will need to test size so a continuous variable can be assigned to each flower (i.e. width/diameter in cm). You should be able to predict other values using the line graph you generate.

What results should I expect?

Some paper will be very absorbent and the flowers will open quickly but the actual results will depend on the paper you provide. The type of paper often has the greatest effect on the speed of opening.

Flowers with many more petals tend to open more slowly.

Smaller flowers tend to open more quickly than larger ones.

When there are more layers, with one flower inside another, it takes a while for the central flower to open as the water has to travel through the outer flowers to reach it. This is why I suggest making a hole in the centre of the outer flower as it lets the water in and speeds up the process but you may choose not to cut a hole. Once you introduce the hole, you introduce a new variable for these flowers so make sure you flag that up to the children as something they should keep the same.

 ## Finale

Once you have packed everything away and looked at the results, decide upon the most absorbent and the least. Tear each paper roughly and place in a dry tray. Use the hand-held digital microscope to look closely at the fibres on the torn edge of the paper.

Now, carefully drip one drop of water onto the tray and get it in view with the microscope. Slide the torn edge of the paper towards the drip. The speed at which the water is absorbed is very different for different papers and this is much more obvious when observed up close.

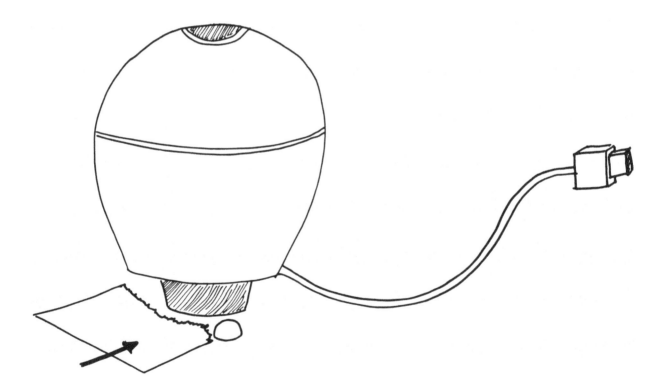

You can talk about the fibres and the spaces between the fibres and the water being attracted to the cellulose fibres. You could use the term 'capillary action' to describe the water moving into the spaces. Once you can see the fibres up close, it is easier to visualise the water moving into these tiny spaces.

What next?

If you want to record your findings in a creative way then you could:

- Write a scientific article for 'Wonderland Gardener's Weekly' explaining to Paper Gardeners how to create a dazzling display of opening roses for the Queen. You can recommend the optimum number of petals (if that's what you tested) to make sure the display is fast and you don't get your head chopped off for delaying the Queen. Or you could recommend the best type of paper (red of course) for a nice quick display of blooms. Explain the test you did and share your results to support your advice.

- Write a letter to the Queen, persuading her that paper flowers might be more reliable than the real thing. Make sure you explain what they are and how they work, as well as letting her know why they might be better than real flowers (e.g. gardeners won't get the colour wrong, they take much less maintenance, can bloom at any time of year, you can change your mind about the colour very easily, etc.).

- Write and perform an advert for paper flowers. Explain how they work and use your results to show which colour/size/design gives the fastest results. You could be in role as Alice or a playing card gardener.

Assessing children's understanding

The following statements are indicators of basic understanding:

- The flowers made of sugar paper opened the fastest.
- The sugar paper absorbed the water the fastest.
- The big flowers opened more slowly.
- The flowers with lots of petals opened more slowly than those with fewer petals.

More advanced understanding:

- The paper absorbs water because water is drawn into the tiny spaces by capillary action.
- The flower unfolds as the paper swells up with the water it has absorbed and the creases are flattened out.
- The fluffier fibres and thicker papers provide more space for the water to flow into so they are more absorbent.
- Some paper is designed to be less absorbent, e.g. writing paper is not very absorbent so ink doesn't spread and go blurry.

Patterns they may be able to describe:

- The bigger the flower the more slowly it opened.
- The more petals the flower had the more slowly it opened.

Science skills

Remember to look out for **evidence of planning an investigation and controlling variables and plotting bar charts or line graphs.**

This is a good investigation for checking that the children are changing only one variable. There are so many variables here and such a temptation to just try something that is pretty, without thinking about what you are testing. I generally let the children have a go at cutting out flowers, folding and floating them first and then remind them to change only one variable.

At this point, I ask them to describe or hold up the two flowers they plan to compare, e.g. large red sugar paper vs medium sized red sugar paper, and let the rest of the class check the other variables are the same, e.g. number of petals etc. You won't need to check everyone at this stage as you can go round and watch them and talk to them about their choices but it serves as a good reminder and gets them back on task once they've learned how to make the flowers for themselves.

References

Carroll, L. (1865). *Alice's Adventures in Wonderland*. London: Macmillan.

Carroll, L. (2009). *Alice's Adventures in Wonderland and Through the Looking-Glass and What Alice Found There*, ed. H. Haughton. London: Penguin Classics.

Coates, D., and Wilson, H. (2003). *Challenges in Primary Science: Meeting the Needs of Able Young Scientists at Key Stage 2*. London: NACE/Fulton Publication.

Dahl, R. (1964). *Charlie and the Chocolate Factory*. New York: A.A. Knopf.

Johnston, J. (2004). The value of exploration and discovery. *Primary Science Review* (85), 21–3.

Leathers, P. (2013). *The Black Rabbit*. London: Walker Books.

Morpurgo, M. (1999). *Kensuke's Kingdom*. London: Egmont.

Pullman, P. (1995). *The Northern Lights*. London: Scholastic UK.

Royal Society of Chemistry. (n.d.). *Mission: Starlight – A global experiment on UV protection*. From The Royal Society of Chemistry: www.rsc.org

Smith, C., and Pottle, J. (2015). *Science Through Stories*. Stroud, UK: Hawthorn Press.

The Royal Institution. (n.d.). *Giant bubbles – science with children – ExpeRimental #3*. From The Royal Institution: www.rigb.org

The Science Museum. (n.d.). *Rocket Mice*. From Science Museum: www.sciencemuseum.org.uk

Torday, P. (2013). *The Last Wild*. London: Quercus Children's Books.

Watson, J. (1968). *The Double Helix*. New York: Athenaeum Press.

Useful websites

BBC Bitesize: www.bbc.com/education

BBSRC Clippy Island: www.bbsrc.ac.uk/engagement/schools/keystage3/natural-selection/

Jon Wood: www.jonwoodscience.com/

Royal Institution (bubbles): www.rigb.org/families/experimental/giant-bubbles

Sarah Bearchell: www.bearchell.co.uk

The Woodland Trust: www.woodlandtrust.org.uk

Index